DISCOVER THE
GREAT BARRIER REEF
MARINE PARK

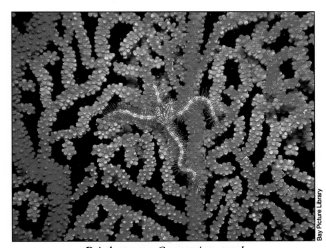

Bay Picture Library

Brittlestar on Gorgonian coral.

Kev Deacon/Dive 2000

COVER: *Snorkelling on the Reef (photograph by Ron and Val Taylor)*

COVER INSET: *Diver feeding a school of Sergeant Major fish — with a Batfish in foreground (photograph by Kev Deacon/DIVE 2000)*

A BAY BOOKS PUBLICATION
An imprint of HarperCollinsPublishers

First published in Australia in 1989
This revised edition published in 1992

Bay Books, of
CollinsAngus&Robertson Publishers Pty Limited
A division of HarperCollinsPublishers (Australia) Pty Limited
25 Ryde Road, Pymble NSW 2073, Australia

Copyright text © Great Barrier Reef Marine Park Authority

This book is copyright.
Apart from any fair dealing for the purposes of private study, research, criticism or review, as permitted under the Copyright Act, no part may be reproduced by any process without written permission. Inquiries should be addressed to the publishers.

National Library of Australia
Card number and ISBN 1 86378 090 4.

Designed by Ivy Hansen
Typesetting by Savage Type Pty Ltd, Brisbane
Printed in Australia by Griffin Press

5 4 3 2 1
95 94 93 92

Acknowledgements
The publishers wish to thank the following for their assistance: Lesley Murdoch, Education and Information Section, Great Barrier Reef Marine Park Authority, for coordinating and compiling this book; Don Alcock, Fiona Alongi, Jean Dartnall, Elaine Eager, Andrew Elliott, Jane Hardie, Graeme Kelleher, Geoff Kelly, Don Kinsey, Brian Lassig, David Lawrence, Simon Lyas, Ray Neale, Calvin Tilley and Leon Zann for their contributions and advice.

The publishers also wish to thank Ansett Airlines.

Illustrations by
Geoff Kelly (pages 18, 21, 22, 32, 38, 40, 41)
and Kevan Hardacre (pages 28–29)

Yellow and pink gorgonia corals. These gorgonia corals grow in protected, low light situations with good current flow.

DISCOVER THE

GREAT BARRIER REEF

MARINE PARK

Compiled by
LESLEY MURDOCH
Great Barrier Reef Marine Park Authority

Gorgonia and balloon fish.

1 THE WONDER DOWN UNDER

From the moon it looks like a white line in the blue-green ocean, from an aircraft it resembles a never-ending tapestry along the Queensland coast, and from the surface of the sea itself the Great Barrier Reef is seen to be one of nature's most remarkable living structures.

This eighth 'natural' wonder of the world is a brightly coloured kaleidoscope of hundreds of different corals and thousands of sea creatures that have developed amazing roles and relationships in adapting to their unique coral reef habitat.

Reef poet Mark O'Connor describes its creation as a technicolour Garden of Eden under the sea.

> . . . In conclusion, I want,
> he said,
> ten thousand mixed chains of
> predation — none of your simple
> rabbit and coyote stuff!
> This ocean shall have many
> mouths, many palates, many
> means of ingestion. I want
> a hundred means of death, and
> three thousand of birth —
> all in technicolour naturally. And
> oh yes,
> I nearly forgot
> we can use Eden again for the
> small coral cay in the centre.

A blue angel fish, just one of the 1500 fish species found in the Great Barrier Reef region, hides among the coral that provides both its food and its shelter.
INSET: A hermit crab of the genus Dardanus searches a coral bommie at night for food, its soft abdomen protected in a shell which has been discarded by its original builder.

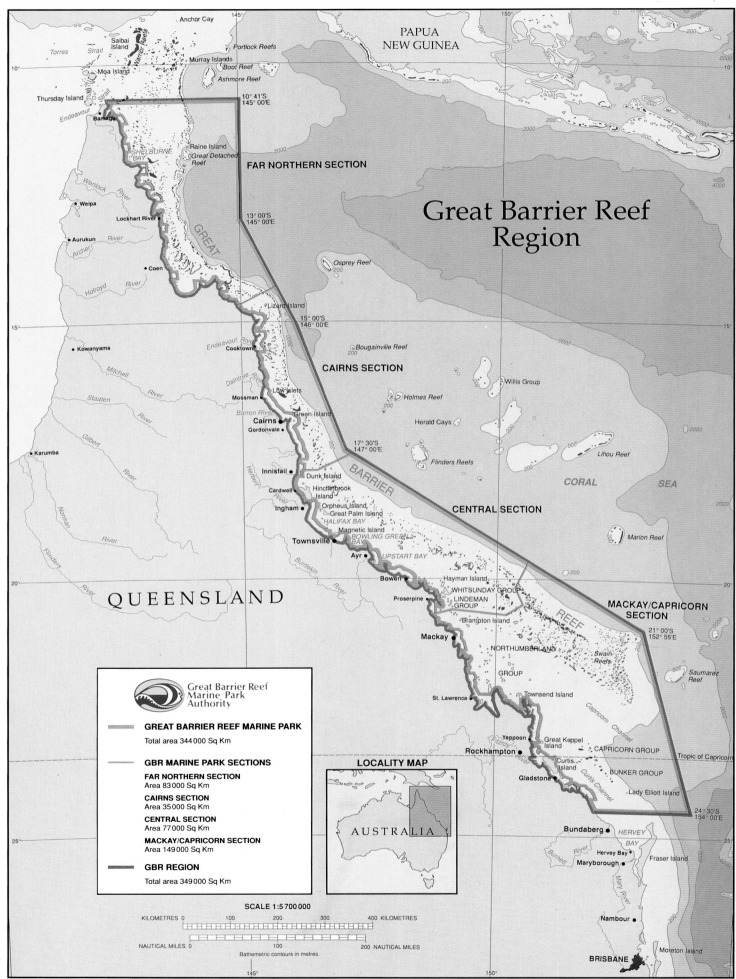

Great Barrier Reef Region

PAPUA NEW GUINEA

FAR NORTHERN SECTION

CAIRNS SECTION

CENTRAL SECTION

MACKAY/CAPRICORN SECTION

QUEENSLAND

CORAL SEA

GREAT BARRIER REEF

Great Barrier Reef Marine Park Authority

GREAT BARRIER REEF MARINE PARK
Total area 344 000 Sq Km

GBR MARINE PARK SECTIONS

FAR NORTHERN SECTION
Area 83 000 Sq Km

CAIRNS SECTION
Area 35 000 Sq Km

CENTRAL SECTION
Area 77 000 Sq Km

MACKAY/CAPRICORN SECTION
Area 149 000 Sq Km

GBR REGION
Total area 349 000 Sq Km

LOCALITY MAP

AUSTRALIA

SCALE 1:5 700 000

KILOMETRES 0   100   200   300   400 KILOMETRES

NAUTICAL MILES 0   100   200 NAUTICAL MILES

Bathymetric contours in metres.

BRA Q 187 1992

COMPILED from information obtained from various larger scale maps.
PROJECTION: Simple conic with two standard parallels 15°S and 20°S

What is the Great Barrier Reef?

This seaward barrier which stretches along the north-eastern coast of Australia is the largest complex of coral reefs and islands in the world. It has more than 2900 individual reefs and about 900 islands, including small, bare sand cays, permanent vegetated cays and many continental islands. It covers an area greater than that of Victoria or Britain and is half the size of Texas.

The Reef is the home of an astonishing diversity and abundance of life forms. There are about 400 different types of hard and soft corals, about 4000 molluscs (clams, snails and their kin), and thousands of different sponges, worms, crustaceans (crabs, shrimps and their relatives), echinoderms (starfish, sea urchins, sea cucumbers and their relatives) and other, less familiar, creatures. This immense variety of invertebrate life forms provides a backdrop to some 1500 species of fish of all descriptions.

The Reef is also the breeding area for a number of rare and endangered animal species. Humpback whales come from the Antarctic to give birth to their young in Reef waters. Six of the world's seven species of sea turtle breed on the Reef, and dugong make their home among the sheltered seagrass beds.

For some people the Great Barrier Reef is their livelihood. Reef waters, which support an abundance of fish and seafood, sustain an important commercial fishing industry in Queensland.

The Reef region is one of Australia's major tourist destinations. The advent of high-speed, large-capacity catamarans now provides tourists with access to areas of the Reef which were once only visited by a privileged few. Whether snorkelling, diving or catching a fish for the family table, the Reef is a marvellous place for recreation.

For shipping or pleasure craft, the Great Barrier Reef can be a formidable obstacle to navigation. In most places the Reef is many kilometres from the coast, but the waters within the outer barrier are also studded with submerged shoals and reefs. Added to this are the strong trade winds and occasional cyclones which are characteristic of the region. Sailing the Barrier Reef is often a test of navigational skill.

To scientists, the Reef is a place of never-ending fascination. They study its weather, its water currents, its geology, its chemistry and its plants and animals, in an attempt to discover how this amazing system works.

BELOW: *The underside of a rock often presents an amazing range of creatures. Here, nudibranchs creep among encrusting animals. Most of the nudibranchs, also called sea slugs, are brightly coloured. Some have skin glands that secrete toxic chemicals, while others accumulate the stinging cells of their coelenterate prey. The colours may remind predators that they are unpleasant to eat.*

ABOVE: *Sponges often grow over the lower surface of rocks forming a colourful mosaic. Here they are living in company with a group of anemones which spread their tentacles to catch small animals.*

RIGHT: *The clarity of Barrier Reef waters provides wonderful experiences for divers but is also essential for the survival of the Reef itself. Many human activities result in pollution or sediment that can dim this clarity with serious consequences for the Reef community. The Great Barrier Reef Marine Park is managed to ensure that wisdom is exercised in the use of the region.*

S.C. Brown/G.B.R.M.P.A.

10

A World Heritage Site

In its nomination of the Great Barrier Reef for inclusion on the World Heritage List, the Australian Government said:

The Great Barrier Reef is by far the largest single collection of coral reefs in the world. Biologically the Great Barrier Reef supports the most diverse ecosystem known to man. Its enormous diversity is thought to reflect the maturity of an ecosystem which has evolved over millions of years on the north-east continental shelf of Australia.

Mike Rowland

K. Atkinson/G.B.R.M.P.A.

LEFT: *Not all the beautiful creatures of the Reef are big or obvious. These tiny creatures float in the surface waters, part of the plankton. Their colour blends with the blue of the sea surface and may protect them from predatory birds. Glaucus is a nudibranch, a mollusc without a shell. Its expanded 'arms' help it keep afloat. Porpita is a colonial hydrozoan. The disc contains air bubbles to keep the animals afloat.*

ABOVE: *The depth of this shell midden on Nagi Island speaks of the long time during which Aborigines and Torres Strait Islanders have collected their food from these waters. The importance of its archaeological sites and the Reef's place in modern Aboriginal life were supporting reasons for its World Heritage status.*

BELOW: *The sea urchin is well protected by spines. Its mouth is on the underside of the body, surrounded by five strong teeth used to scrape algae from the rocks.*

G.B.R.M.P.A.

ABOVE: *Most World Heritage sites need only one plaque but the Great Barrier Reef is so large that a number of plaques have been produced and placed in prominent places throughout the Reef region.*

ABOVE: *Anemone fish rest safely in their anemone, which would be deadly to other fish their size. They produce a thick mucus coating which protects them from the stinging cells of the anemone.*

The Great Barrier Reef provides some of the most spectacular scenery on earth and is a major feeding ground for large populations of the endangered species *Dugong dugon*. The Reef contains nesting grounds of world significance for the endangered green turtle (*Chelonia mydas*) and loggerhead turtle (*Caretta caretta*), and also contains many middens and other archaeological sites of Aboriginal or Torres Strait Islander origin. There are many historic shipwrecks in the area, and on the islands, many of which are Queensland National Parks, there are ruins and operating lighthouses which are of cultural and historical significance.

In recognition of its outstanding universal value, the Great Barrier Reef was inscribed on the World Heritage List on 26 October 1981.

12

The Great Barrier Reef is a marine park and a World Heritage site partly because it provides a home for many species in danger of extinction elsewhere.

LEFT: *In many parts of the world turtles are endangered, but the Reef provides calm and protected waters for turtle mating and safe sandy islands for egg laying.*

ABOVE: *Although the dugong is endangered throughout much of its range, the Reef supports substantial populations.*

BELOW: *Humpback whales used to be hunted in Australian waters. Now they are fully protected and are becoming a frequent sight during their annual migrations. Each winter they leave the Antarctic to mate and give birth in Barrier Reef waters.*

Caring for the Reef

The Great Barrier Reef region is administered by the Great Barrier Reef Marine Park Authority. The day-to-day management of this Marine Park is undertaken by the Queensland Department of Environment and Heritage.

In keeping with the spirit of the World Heritage Convention, the primary goal of the Authority is to provide for the protection, wise use, understanding and enjoyment of the Great Barrier Reef in perpetuity through the development and care of the Marine Park.

The concept of the Marine Park is based on a balance between conservation of the Reef and its prolific animal and plant life, and reasonable use by fishermen, collectors, charter operators, tourists, scientists and others.

To achieve this balance the Marine Park Authority has developed zoning plans which define the type of activities which may take place on different parts of the Reef.

LEFT: *Marine Park rangers like to share their enthusiasm for the Reef with others. Through education and understanding, the care and protection of the Reef can become the concern of everyone who uses it.*

LEFT: *An aerial view gives a new perspective on a coral reef. This is part of the coral gardens of the Swain Reefs complex in the southern part of the Great Barrier Reef. Such outer reefs are less easy to reach from land and may be zoned to allow for fewer activities.*

TOP LEFT: *Marine Park management is really the management of people using the Reef. Rangers encourage an interest in, and appreciation of the Reef in visitors of all ages. Tourists may unwittingly cause damage or put themselves in danger. Rangers provide help and advice to prevent this.*

ABOVE: *Reef walking at low tide is one of the best ways to see a range of Reef creatures, especially for the non-diver. A walk guided by a Marine Park ranger is particularly valuable. Strong footwear and good sun protection are essential. Rocks must always be replaced after inspection to protect the creatures living underneath from predators, sunlight and drying out.*

BELOW: *Management of the Barrier Reef involves knowing about the resource being managed. A ranger's day does not always finish at sunset and may include a variety of work. Here rangers load a boat with equipment for a night dive.*

15

2 REEFS, ISLANDS AND CORAL CAYS

Flying over the north Queensland coast you can see that the Reef is not one impenetrable barrier but a collection of thousands of different reefs and islands, many of which had their origins as far back as the last ice age.

Today, some of these islands are popular tourist resorts whilst others are preserved in their natural state, inhabited only by wildlife.

Natural Images/A.N.T. Photo Library

Kev Deacon/Dive 2000

Green Island is a coral cay on a large platform reef, not far from the coastal city of Cairns. Most of the island is a national park but it also supports a popular tourist resort. The National Park and the Marine Park surrounding the island are managed in a complementary way to ensure that the continuous ecosystem of island and reef are used appropriately.
LEFT: Casuarinas are often found on Reef island beach edges.
RIGHT: Pickersgill Reef from the air shows an unvegetated mobile sand cay. The darker blue of the deep water contrasts with the turquoise of the shallows and the extent of coral growth can be seen clearly.

L Zell/GBRMPA

The Birth and Growth of the Reef

Reefs have grown on the continental shelf of Queensland for about two million years in the south, and as much as eighteen million years in the north.

The sea level has changed many times over the years. In the last ice age it dropped dramatically to 100 metres below its current level — draining the continental shelf and exposing reefs as coastal limestone hills. In those days it would have been possible to walk out to the outer Reef.

About 20 000 years ago the last ice age ended and the sea, replenished by melting ice caps, rose rapidly. About 10 000 years ago the sea began to flood the old limestone hills for the first time in more than 100 000 years. Corals grew on old eroded reef platforms to form the reefs of today's Great Barrier Reef. The sea reached its present level approximately 6000 years ago.

Reef Shapes and Sizes

There is a bewildering range of reefs and islands on the Great Barrier Reef. However, the most common are ribbon reefs, fringing reefs and patch reefs.

Ribbon reefs occur in the northern part. They are relatively narrow walls on the edge of the continental shelf and form a broken barrier with passages between individual reefs. Some of these passages are large enough to allow ships through.

Fringing reefs develop off the sloping sides of continental islands or along the mainland coast. Patch reefs are usually round or oval and grow like platforms on the continental shelf.

Reef shapes develop in response to particular combinations of geological, meteorological and biological conditions.

Coral Cays

A coral cay is a 'low' island formed entirely from the sedimentary debris created by the reef on which it stands, sediments which have been swept into a particular part of the reef by wave action. No continental rocks are associated with coral cays which are thus clearly differentiated from the 'high' islands with fringing reefs usually found closer to the mainland.

Origins of the Reef

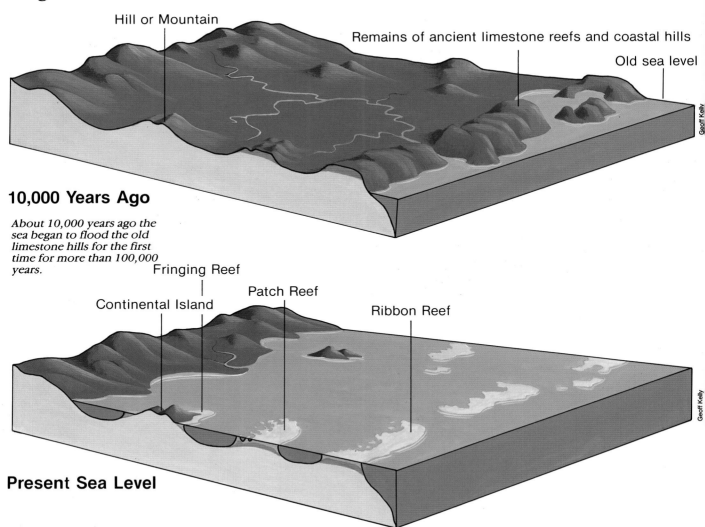

Hill or Mountain

Remains of ancient limestone reefs and coastal hills

Old sea level

Geoff Kelly

10,000 Years Ago

About 10,000 years ago the sea began to flood the old limestone hills for the first time for more than 100,000 years.

Fringing Reef

Continental Island

Patch Reef

Ribbon Reef

Present Sea Level

Geoff Kelly

18

ABOVE: *Hardy Reef in the Central Section of the Marine Park.*
RIGHT: *Ribbon reefs are characteristic of the part of the Reef north of Cairns. Where they are widely spaced there may be navigable channels between them, but when they are close together the sea boils dangerously through the narrow gaps at change of tide.*

How the Cay is Formed

As the plants and animals which form and live on a coral reef die, the smaller skeletons and debris are swept by waves towards the leeside of the reef. Larger coral boulders and particularly shingle, formed mainly from the broken sticks of branching corals, may be deposited closer to the windward side of the reef. However, unless the sweeping action of the waves concentrates the debris into a particular part of the reef flat, no island can form. Instead, as is the case on many reefs, only a scattered area of rubble occurs on the windward side of the reef, grading into a sand sheet to the lee.

Sometimes the shape of a reef and its orientation to the prevailing waves results in bending or refraction of the wave fronts as they move into the shallow waters of the reef flat. This causes the sand or shingle to be swept into a particular part of the reef flat. This concentration of sediment is the initial stage in cay formation. A large area of reef flat is not necessary for cays to form and some form on small patches no larger than a football field.

L. Zell/G.B.R.M.P.A.

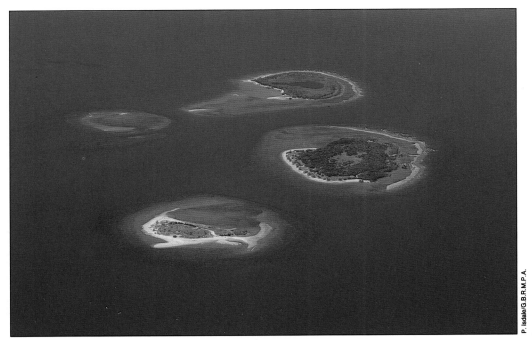

LEFT: *The Turtle Group are well-developed cays in the Cairns Section of the Marine Park. They carry vegetation including a tree zone. Although this stabilises the cays, beaches may still move a good deal under the influence of wind and wave.* OPPOSITE: *Hoskyn Reef, in the Mackay/Capricorn section of the Marine Park carries a vegetated cay.*

P. Isdale/G.B.R.M.P.A.

The Cay develops

Initially, the embryo cay is little more than an unstable sand bank, changing its position on the reef flat by tens of metres with every change in weather conditions. As it increases in size, however, such movements become smaller and, while changes to the shape of the cay may still take place, its position on the reef becomes more stable. King tides build it up to levels which are overlapped only a few times a year and seabirds begin to nest on its crown.

These birds bring in seeds of plants, either attached to their feathers or in droppings. Many of the early colonising plants of cays have seeds which float and are still capable of germination when washed up after as much as 90 days at sea. This initial vegetation is usually in the form of low creepers which help to stabilise the sand surface. The young island has a dune capping which could rise above the highest tides.

. . . and stabilises

The colonising vegetation adds organic matter to the raw sands of the cay and the developing sandy soils may also be enriched by the phosphatic guano from nesting seabirds. In time, rainfall carries the guano down into the cay where phosphates cement the cay sands into a hard pan known as cay sandstone. Some cays of the Great Barrier Reef were mined for this source of phosphate towards the end of the last century, and the excavated pits are still clearly visible on these islands.

The cay sandstone further stabilises the cay against movement or erosion. Beach rock, formed when calcium carbonate precipitates out of the ground waters of the cay, cements sub-surface beach deposits together. The cemented deposits form a concrete-like ramp which acts as a very effective buffer against erosion.

. . . but is still vulnerable

Once the cay exceeds an area of a few hectares, a freshwater lens — a small natural reservoir of ground water — may form beneath the cay. This allows other plants, particularly trees, to become established.

However, no cay can be regarded as completely stable. Changes are constantly taking place, particularly at the narrower ends of cays where unvegetated spits may alter position on almost every tide. A tropical cyclone could completely erode even a large cay with beach rock; several reefs in the Great Barrier Reef show outlines where this has happened.

Coral Reef Cays are geologically young

Coral reef cays developed only in the last 6000 years or so since sea level rose to its present position from its low stand of the last great ice age. Only when the sea level stabilised was it possible for reef flats to expand and provide potential sites for the formation of cays.

Cays are not uniformly distributed over the Great Barrier Reef. Vegetated shingle cays are found only on southern reefs open to the Tasman Sea's oceanic swells. Low wooded islands are found only north of Cairns and close to the mainland because their development requires small wave movement and colonisation by mangroves from the nearby mainland.

Vegetated sand cays are found only on the northern Great Barrier Reef north of Cairns (Green Island is the southernmost of this group) and on the southern Reef south of Mackay. The entire central Great Barrier Reef, for a distance of 640 kilometres has no vegetated cays and few unvegetated ones. This is probably because the shape of many reefs in this area does not allow waves to build up debris. Also tropical cyclones, which can scatter concentrated sediments over a reef flat, reach their greatest strength and frequency on the central Reef. In addition, the tidal range on the Great Barrier Reef is greatest in the south central region, a factor which acts against sediments being deposited in a particular area.

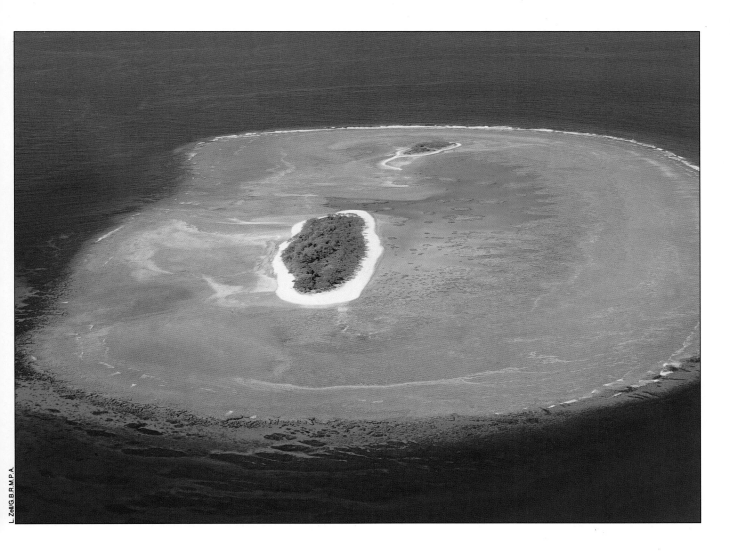

L. Zell/G.B.R.M.P.A.

Reef profile

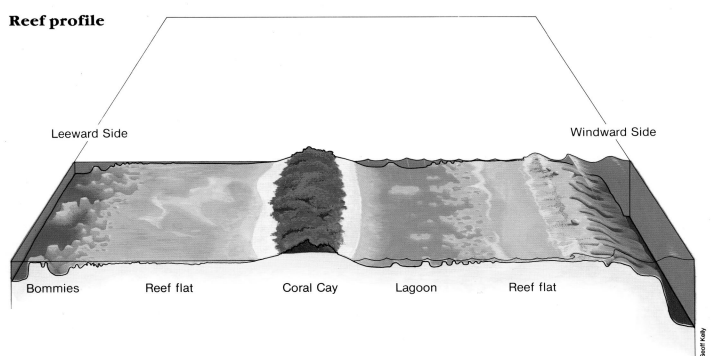

Leeward Side

Windward Side

Bommies   Reef flat   Coral Cay   Lagoon   Reef flat

Geoff Kelly

21

Fringing Reefs

Fringing reefs are coral structures attached to the mainland or to continental high islands. In the Great Barrier Reef region most fringing reefs are found around continental islands, particularly in Reef waters north of Mackay. As many of the Barrier Reef resorts are located on such islands, fringing reefs are probably the reef type most commonly seen by visitors.

Natural Images/A.N.T. Photo Library

ABOVE: *This is a mainland fringing reef in the area near Mossman, north of Cape Tribulation, where the rainforest grows almost down to the sea. Sediment in run-off from the land is a problem for mainland fringing reefs. The amount of run-off and the material it carries is influenced by land use.*
RIGHT: *Lizard Island and its satellites, Eagle Island and South Island, are continental islands, not coral cays. That is, they are outliers of the mainland and share a similar geology. These islands are surrounded by extensive fringing reefs. Most of the land visible in this picture is National Park, but Lizard Island also supports a tourist resort and a marine research station operated by the Australian Museum in Sydney.*

Cross section of a fringing reef

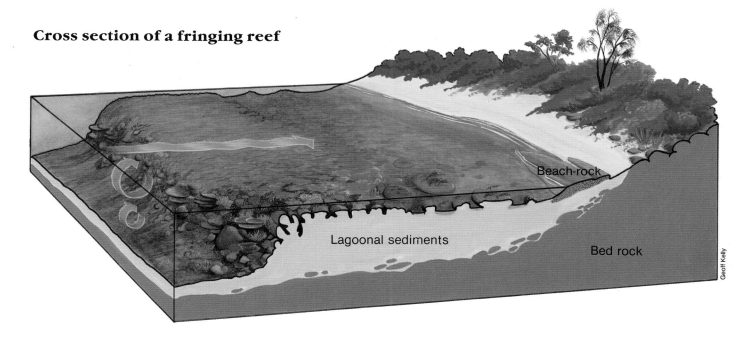

Beach-rock

Lagoonal sediments

Bed rock

Geoff Kelly

Where Are the Fringing Reefs?

Fringing reefs extend much further south than the outer reefs. The early stages of these reefs are found as far south as the Solitary Islands offshore from Coffs Harbour in New South Wales. Wide fringing reefs off Lord Howe Island in the northern Tasman Sea are the southernmost reefs in the world.

Mainland fringing reefs are limited in the Barrier Reef region. The large amounts of sediment and fresh water which the coastal rivers deliver to the nearshore area are harmful to coral growth. Two easily accessible mainland reefs, King Reef near Kurrimine in the Tully district and Alexander Reef between Cairns and Port Douglas, both have a heavy sediment cover. Consequently, most corals are found on the reef slopes rather than the reef flats. Narrow but more extensive fringing reefs are found in the Cape Tribulation area and on the rocky sections of coastline north of Cooktown.

Fringing reefs are found around the majority of offshore islands (except Hinchinbrook Island) where the waters are much clearer than those close to the mainland. Around rocky headlands fringing reefs may be continuous but narrow, often no more than 20 metres wide. However, many of the bays of the islands on both windward and leeward sides have much wider reefs extending right across their mouths. Many smaller islands have reefs 500 metres or more in width, extending as pear-shaped extensions on their leeward sides. Sand spits constructed from island sands frequently extend across the reef flat. On Dunk Island, for example, the resort is located on such a sand spit.

On the far northern Great Barrier Reef continental islands or isolated rock outcrops are found even among the outer reefs, which are much closer to the mainland. Fringing reefs are larger and more complex. The fringing reef at Lizard Island, for example, includes a deep lagoon and in many respects is similar to the outer reefs. In some instances, a fringing reef has an area many times greater than the island or rock which it surrounds.

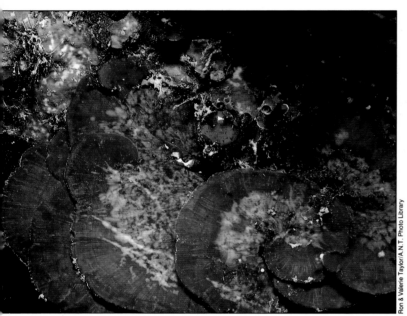

What Do Fringing Reefs Look Like?

To many people the emergence of a fringing reef at low tide is a disappointment. The inner reef is sometimes entirely covered by sand or mud. Much of the central reef flat is dominated by plants rather than the expected corals. Only towards the outer edge of the reef do living corals dominate and a surprising variety may be found.

Even greater species diversity is found on the reef front where massive colonies of the coral *Porites* form 'bommies' up to eight metres high and several metres in diameter.

Seaweed and Plant Life

Seaweed known as *Sargassum* is common on the reef fronts. On more exposed windward fringing reefs, the reef crest is often encrusted by a pinkish limestone-secreting plant.

In shallow water among the rubble, an alga consisting of dark green runners with small grape-like clusters binds the coral rubble. In moated pools grow extensive swards of the delicate fan-like funnel weed with its brown star-shaped tips. Flat, almost featureless reef tops often support a cover of low turf-like plants. These form small steps or rimmed pools towards the outer edge of the reef. Seagrasses occur in the sandy inner reef flats; mangroves are found in muddier areas.

Protecting the Fringing Reefs

The fringing reefs of the Great Barrier Reef are the most accessible to visitors and are therefore the most vulnerable to human activities.

It is clear from photographs taken over 80 years ago by the photographer and naturalist, W. Saville Kent, that the variety of corals on many reefs has declined since then. Some may have been damaged by cyclones and the excessive amounts of fresh water and silt which accompany such storms.

Land-use practices on the mainland can intensify the problems of freshwater run-off and siltation. As more land is cleared of its protective natural vegetation, stormwater run-off becomes more rapid and intense and soil erosion increases. Agricultural fertilisers, sewage and other city wastes, often part of storm run-off, have severe adverse effects on reefs.

TOP: *North Direction Island is another continental island surrounded by fringing reef.*
ABOVE: *Rocky shores support many species of red algae like that shown here. The round ball is another alga, Valonia, which is sometimes described as looking like ball bearings and has the picturesque common name, sailor's eyeballs.*
BELOW: *Calcareous algae form an important part of the Reef structure. Their name describes the texture which is chalky or stony because algae contain a lot of lime. Red calcareous algae can withstand the waves and are often well developed on the outermost parts of reefs where they are more successful at reef-building than the corals.*

G.B.R.M.P.A.

Ivy Hansen

ABOVE: *The Whitsunday Group has many types of reef habitat. Shown here is a continental island with fringing reef and a platform reef with some cay formation.*

LEFT: *Many plants have developed adaptations that allow them to grow in muddy, saline conditions at the sea edge. They form the mangrove community. Prop roots provide physical support for plants in this unstable environment, while aerial roots allow respiration, which can be a problem in waterlogged soil. Many mangroves have thick, fleshy leaves which help to limit the evaporation of precious fresh water.*

25

3 THE REEF COMMUNITY

The Reef is like a big city with many of its inhabitants busy during the day and others coming to life mainly after dark. All live together in a complex ecosystem where hundreds of different plants and animals are dependent on each other for food and survival. There are many unusual partnerships and roles — this diverse world even has its own cleaners and garbage collectors!

Predator-prey relationships are some of the most obvious connections between animals. Butterfly fish use their pointed snouts to feed on coral polyps. Their flattened shape allows them to slip into cracks between coral clumps both to reach food and to escape predators.

TOP INSET: Among these staghorn corals are sea perch, a widespread species that varies a good deal in colour. They are members of the Serranidae family.

BOTTOM INSET: Although this sea moth or dragonfish stands out against a brilliant gorgonian coral, its shape helps to disguise it in its usual weedy habitat.

Another World

Listen to any first-time visitors to a coral reef when they come to the surface after their first look under the water. Unintelligible splutterings through a snorkel: 'Fantastic!' 'Marvellous!' 'Did you see that?'

Reef walkers turning over a coral rock on the reef top are astonished by the variety of organisms underneath: almost certainly a number of different types of colourful encrusting sponges; softer colonial and solitary sea squirts; delicate lace corals or bryozoans; slithering serpent stars and worms; and scores of other colourful and strangely shaped animals.

Perhaps the reef walker may find a pair of glossy cowries, shells enveloped in velvety mantles, or a strikingly coloured cone shell. Specialist shell collectors will certainly appreciate the diversity of shell species: perhaps a hundred different species of cowry and cone shells alone might be found on a single reef.

Those diving along the edge of the reef will be similarly impressed by the great diversity of fish of all shapes, colours and sizes, from tiny bottom-dwelling blennies to giant manta rays. Of the 3000 or so species present in Australian waters, half are to be found on coral reefs.

Many thousands of different types of plants and animals are found on coral reefs. Virtually all major and minor groups of living things are abundantly represented there. Only the tropical rainforests come near to rivalling the coral reef for richness of species.

ABOVE LEFT: *Rather like a squid in a shell, the nautilus is a reminder of its distant ancestors — squids and octopuses. The shell is divided by up to 30 cross connections. The animal lives in the largest, outermost chamber. The inner chambers contain gas which allows the animal to float.*
LEFT: *A giant manta ray,* Manta birostris, *may measure up to 7 metres across the disc. Although they are so large, they are harmless to people. They feed on small fish and plankton and live in open, surface waters between reefs. They swim by graceful undulations of their 'wings' and are famous for their habit of leaping out of the water and falling back with a spectacular splash.*

Living places on a coral reef

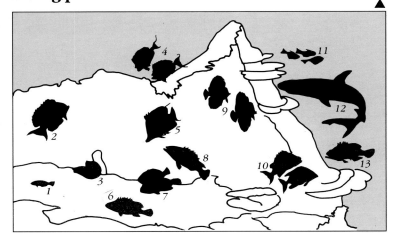

Fish often found on the reef flat, reef crest, and reef front:

1. *Pearl-spotted wrasse* — Halichoeres margaritaceus
2. *Surgeonfish* — Acanthurus *sp.*
3. *Mottled reef eel* — Gymnothorax undulatus
4. *Brown unicorn fish* — Naso unicornus
5. *Threadfin coralfish* — Chaetodon auriga
6. *Honeycomb cod* — Epinephelus merra
7. *Parrotfish* — Scarus *sp.*
8. *Groper* — Promicrops lanceolatus
9. *Purple sailfinned tang* — Zebrasoma veliferum
10. *Red emperor* — Lutjanus sebae
11. *Bulls eyes* — Pempheris oualensis
12. *White-tip shark* — Triaenodon apicalis
13. *Red-spotted coral cod* — Cephalopholis leopardus

Different fish are found in various parts of the Reef according to their needs.

29

The Reef Builders

Corals: the Building Bricks

Coral reefs are composed of mostly 'dead' limestone and only a small part of the surface is alive with colourful coral. Coral reefs are named after the tiny animals called polyps. Polyps are the most obvious reef builders, although the algae are the most important. The coral polyps, by producing a skeleton of limestone and dividing to form new polyps, create the living structures known as coral colonies.

A coral colony is not a group of individuals living together for the common good, but rather the result of growth and division of an original founder polyp. Coral colonies provide the framework around and within which live all sorts of reef animals, such as fish, worms, starfish and molluscs.

Coral colonies grow upwards to the light. They may ultimately reach the surface and die or be ground to rubble in a tropical cyclone. They may be eaten by crown-of-thorns starfish or gradually eroded by borers. If the rate of accumulation of the dead skeletons exceeds the rate of erosion, then a reef is slowly formed.

Although the fast-growing staghorn corals, *Acropora*, may grow as much as 200–300 mm per year, and even the slower-growing massive corals 3–4 mm per year, sediments accumulate on reefs at a rate of only about 1 mm per year.

Reefs are destroyed by heavy seas and chemicals as well as by the creatures of the Reef. Micro-borers such as algae, bacteria and fungi, and macro-borers such as polychaetes and sipunculid worms, bivalve molluscs and sponges erode the dead coral skeletons from within.

A variety of grazers such as parrotfish, snails and sea urchins bite off, rasp or scrape off the external skeleton, while feeding on encrusting algae or extracting the boring organisms within. The skeletons of dead coral are rapidly reduced to rubble and sand. The rubble may be colonised by new coral colonies or redistributed by waves and currents to build the framework of the Reef or create coral islands.

Algae: the Mortar

Although they are inconspicuous on coral reefs, the algae are especially important in reef building. An encrusting coralline alga resembling mauve concrete is of special importance in cementing together the skeletons of corals and other reef creatures and forms a hard pavement on reef crests. In the lagoon and reef slope much of the sediment is composed of button-sized discs of the green alga *Halimeda*, one of the most abundant coral reef algae.

TOP: *One of the atypical molluscs,* Cyerce nigricans *is seen here feeding on turtle weed.*
LEFT: *A two-shell, bivalve mollusc, the file shell,* Promantellum, *can be found on reef flats. It swims about in a jerky fashion.*
ABOVE: *Unlike the other molluscs on this page, clams are immobile once the larvae have settled. This makes them particularly vulnerable to poachers hunting either meat or shells. Clams are fully protected within the Marine Park.*

Corals

The coral polyp has a simple structure. If you are familiar with anemones on the sea shore, you will have an idea of what it looks like. It is a soft cylinder of tissue, closed at the bottom, with a mouth surrounded by tentacles at the top. Inside is an open stomach cavity, partitioned by radiating strips of tissue.

The coral polyp is related to jellyfish and, like these, its tentacles contain tiny stinging cells. It has an external skeleton underneath. During the day, most polyps withdraw into their skeletons, which can then be seen as cylindrical containers called corallites. Polyps in a colony are connected by extensions of their tissues, even of their stomach cavities, so that if one catches food the whole community benefits.

ABOVE: *The mushroom coral, Fungia, is a single large polyp similar in shape to a sea anemone.*
LEFT: *These are the expanded polyps of a faviid coral, one of the brain corals. The mouth of each polyp can be seen in the centre of its tentacles.*

31

How Corals Feed

Corals feed by extending their tentacles armed with stinging cells and catching microscopic floating animals from the waters around them. When the tentacles encounter an animal, such as a shrimp or an early larval stage of some other reef animal, the barbed darts of the stinging cells are fired to paralyse and hold the prey. With a graceful bending motion the tentacle then passes the morsel to the mouth.

The prey is broken down in the polyp's stomach and, through the connections between the polyps, feeds the whole colony. Sometimes corals use nets of mucus to ensnare bacteria and small animals. Organic materials in the sea water passing into the polyp may also supply some nutrient needs.

Hidden Helpers — the Zooxanthellae

The success of corals as reef builders is due largely to a remarkable association with tiny single-celled plants called zooxanthellae which live in the cells of the polyp tissues.

The zooxanthellae, like other plants that photosynthesise, harness energy from sunlight to manufacture materials necessary for their own nutrition and reproduction. In doing so, they make use of carbon dioxide produced by the coral and, in return, they pass some materials back to the coral. Their presence greatly enhances the rate at which polyps create their skeletons.

This mutually beneficial association, called symbiosis, creates supercorals — reef builders — from what would otherwise be insignificant small colonies.

Mark Wellard/A.N.T. Photo Library

ABOVE: *The white-tailed clownfish,* Amphiprion, *is one of the anemone fish. Like many other coral reef fish, this group habitually changes sex. They start as males and become female if there is no female in their group.*

Corals are found in most of the world's seas, even in polar waters, but only those which have symbiotic zooxanthellae and live in shallow, warm, tropical waters grow fast enough to form reefs. Coral reefs are therefore found only where the minimum temperature does not drop below about 18°C, and grow fastest where the temperature is around 26°C. As they require light for the algae's photosynthesis, corals grow best in clear, shallow continental shelf waters (less than about 50 m deep), away from river influences.

Sunlight: the source of life on the Reef

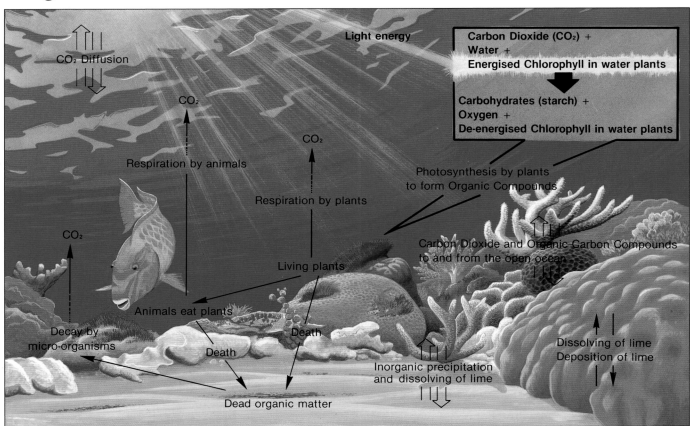

Geoff Kelly

BELOW: *This coral shows bleaching, caused by the coral ejecting some of its zooxanthellae — usually a sign of stress.*
BOTTOM: *Staghorn coral is one growth form of the Acropora species which can also occur as plates, tables, columns or bushes. This variation makes it hard to distinguish one species from another. Acropora is one of the most successful genera of hard coral and is found throughout the world where coral reefs grow. Its success is partly due to a light skeleton which grows quickly and allows it to overcome its neighbours.*

L. Zann

Corals and Light

Although they grow in seas relatively low in nutrients, coral reefs have one of the highest rates of primary production (the production of organic material through photosynthesis) of any natural ecosystem. Daily production is of a similar order to a lush, regularly fertilised sugarcane crop.

Light is filtered rapidly even in crystal clear ocean waters. In deeper waters the zooxanthellae adapt by producing more chlorophyll pigment, but there is insufficient light for photosynthesis below 80 m, even in the clearest of waters.

Paradoxically the zooxanthellae are more efficient, not on the surface, but at rather low light levels, between 10–20 m depths. On the surface and in shallow waters corals and other animals have the problem of too much ultraviolet light (like sunbathers). However, like sunbathers, they use a UV sunscreen. The discovery of new UV blocking agents by scientists at the Australian Institute of Marine Science has tremendous potential not only for sun worshippers but also for the paints and plastics industries.

Corals may still get sunburnt and die. 'Bleaching' occurs when corals are stressed and eject their zooxanthellae. Fresh water, high temperatures, silt, pollution and diseases have this effect, but it seems that high temperatures and light cause massive coral death.

A Diversity of Shapes and Sizes

Coral colonies occur in a great variety of shapes and sizes. The general appearance of the colony depends on the way individual polyps build their skeletons and how they bud off new polyps. A mushroom coral, for example, is a single enormous polyp whose skeleton shows the central position of the mouth with radiating divisions (called septa), giving the appearance of an upturned mushroom with the stalk plucked off.

In the brain corals, polyps divide without forming complete walls, so that long lines of polyps have a common wall around them. Staghorn corals have branches formed by one single polyp growing longer and longer, budding off new polyps around its top as it extends. In many corals, the polyps (or their skeletons, the corallites) can be easily seen, but some corals have tiny polyps which are barely visible to the naked eye.

The shape of the colony is further moulded by influences such as wave action, currents and the exposure of the colony at low tide. Corals living at the waveswept edge of the reef, for example, have a generally lower, sturdier form than those living in sheltered reef lagoons.

The colour of reef-building corals comes from pigments in the tissues of the polyps. When a coral colony dies (for example, when it is taken out of the sea), only its white limestone skeleton remains.

How Corals Reproduce

Coral polyps reproduce sexually by producing sperm and eggs which unite to form tiny rounded larvae called planulae. In some corals, separate colonies have either all male or all female polyps. More often each polyp is both male and female, and releases a bundle of eggs and sperm into the sea water on only one or two nights each year. Many corals reproduce this way on the same nights each year in late spring or early summer. In a few corals, eggs are fertilised inside the polyps, and planulae are brooded to be released over long periods.

The tiny planulae float in the surface waters for a short time, then each swims down to find a suitable spot on the hard reef surface where it will change into a polyp and begin the process of forming a colony.

Because they are made up of many polyps, coral colonies can also reproduce asexually; that is, parts of the colony which break off can survive as separate colonies. This type of reproduction is especially useful in places where there is not much solid space for the settlement of planulae, such as the sandy floors of reef lagoons.

Bette Willis/James Cook University

Corals release egg and sperm masses during spawning. The bundles float to the surface and break up. After fertilisation, the larvae float on the sea surface for a while before settling in another area.
ABOVE LEFT: Acropora
ABOVE: Favites
BELOW: Goniastrea

35

Coral Growth — a Record of Past Climate

In corals which grow as sheets or layers, new polyps are added around the edge of the colony. Branching corals grow by adding new branches as well as extending existing ones. In dome-shaped colonies, new polyps are added within the surface of the dome. As the colony grows, polyps pull themselves upwards and lay down a new 'floor' of skeleton. The living tissues thus 'ride' on top of the accumulating skeleton, occupying only the outer 5–10 mm of the often very large colony.

The skeletons of dome-shaped colonies show annual growth layers which provide a calendar, rather like the rings in a tree trunk. The layers show up as pairs of alternating light and dark bands in an X-ray of a slice cut from the centre of a colony. These bands represent regular, seasonal variations in the density at which the limestone skeleton was deposited on the outer surface of the colony. On the Great Barrier Reef scientists have taken cores from very large colonies and aged them at over 600 years old. They believe the largest colonies observed on the Reef would be about 1200 years old.

The skeletons have banding patterns which show fluorescence related to land-based organic materials that have been incorporated into the skeleton. In areas affected by river outflow fluorescent banding reflects river discharge. By relating patterns to the records of river discharge, the coral skeleton can be used as a diary of past climate. So far, the scientists have been able to extend our knowledge of the climatic trends in the north Queensland region back to the early 1700s.

Kev Deacon/Dive 2000

ABOVE: *The Reef front is the most spectacular diving area. Here, light and water conditions are ideal for corals and many fish are attracted to the abundant growth.*
RIGHT: Caulerpa, *grape weed or sea grapes, is one of the commonest and most variable alga species on the Barrier Reef. It has a creeping axis from which erect branches grow.*

36

Plants: Seaweeds and Seagrasses

The larger 'seaweeds' are conspicuous algae of fringing reef communities closer to the mainland. The fleshy brown *Sargassum* dominates fringing reefs in summer but later it breaks off and drifts away, held afloat by air-filled bladders.

The bright green edible grape seaweed *Caulerpa* and the brilliant green 'turtleweed' *Chlorodesmis* are conspicuous on offshore reef crests and flats, and the coralline green algae *Halimeda* are extremely abundant in deeper lagoons and reef slopes.

Closer to the mainland, pastures of seagrass, a true grass, cover mud flats on sheltered inner shelf reefs and are foraged by turtles, dugong and many fish.

However, the majority of the plants on reefs are very inconspicuous. The coralline 'lithothamnians', which are so important in reef formation, look like concrete or dead coral rock.

The turf algae which are the main food for grazing invertebrates and fish are a nondescript grey-green 'scum' or 'fuzz' covering dead coral. Some of these turf algae have the ability to 'fix' dissolved nitrogen like legume crops on land and the essential nitrates are passed along through the food chain.

Many algae are completely hidden, boring several centimetres into dead coral skeletons.

Ron & Valerie Taylor/A.N.T. Photo Library

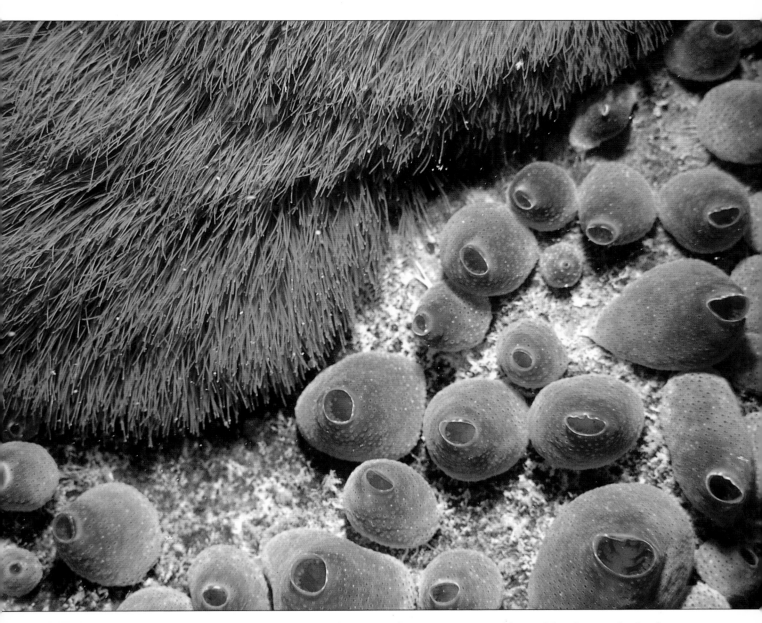

Many of the algae on the Reef are too small to be seen, living inside the cells of animals such as corals and clams. Some green algae, in the form of conventional seaweeds, are found.
ABOVE: Turtle weed, Chlorodesmis is one of the most attractive Barrier Reef algae with its dense green tufts. It is seen here with an ascidian.
LEFT: This alga, Halimeda, is a very important part of the Reef community. It has a limestone skeleton which contributes to reef formation and forms a large part of beach sand and lagoon sediment. Its remains are often found washed up on beaches.

Coral Reef Food Chains

Not so long ago coral reefs were viewed by scientists as animal-dominated systems, fed a plankton soup by the surrounding ocean. Plants did not appear to be very abundant on reefs.

While it is true that some of the nutrients do come from the plankton, coral reefs can thrive like desert oases in plankton-poor oceanic waters. Today marine scientists recognise that most of the energy can be produced on the reef itself and retained in the community by a complex recycling of nutrients.

The energy budget of the coral reef is based on photosynthesis by plants. During photosynthesis plants use carbon dioxide and water to make starch, using sunlight for power. The plant also needs nutrients (fertilisers like the nitrates, phosphates and trace elements that you put on your garden).

The organic carbon manufactured by the plants enters the food chain by a number of paths. Some of the algae are consumed by herbivorous plankton and bottom-dwelling grazing invertebrates, fish and turtles.

These may, in turn, be eaten by other animals, the carnivores. Wastes and the dead remains of plants and animals are ultimately consumed by bacteria, which are in turn an important food source for the filter feeders, such as sponges and clams.

Like burning petrol to make a car run, the process is inefficient, losing about 90 per cent of the energy with each step or link of the food chain. However, many coral reef animals have developed far more efficient 'motors' by taking carbohydrates directly from the living plants, bypassing the wasteful processes of having to capture, consume and digest their food. The process is more like that of a solar-powered engine than of a petrol motor.

BELOW: *A flatworm creeps among the encrusting algae and sponges. Flatworms have a simpler body organisation than segmented worms. The mouth is on the underside and the animals are carnivorous, actively seeking any creature small enough to be overpowered.*

38

A simplified coral reef food chain

1. Microscopic plants ⎫
2. Microscopic animals ⎭ the plankton
3. Spanish mackerel ⎫
4. Coral trout ⎭ the carnivores
5. Butterfly fish ⎫
6. Parrotfish ⎭ the grazers
7. Herrings — the plankton feeders

RIGHT: *This odd-looking thing is two quite different animals —a sponge and some sea anemones. The tubes are exhalant funnels of a sponge, the rest of its surface being covered by sea anemones.*

BELOW: *A school of gold-striped goat fish, Mulloidichthys. Goat fish are named for their beard of two bristles, actually sense organs.*

Plant–Animal Partnerships

Unlike a tropical rainforest and most other ecosystems, the plants on a coral reef are generally not obvious because they often live **in** the animals. The stony corals, the soft corals and giant clams host the microscopic zooxanthellae, the dinoflagellate *Symbiodinium microadriaticum*; while the sponges and colonial sea squirts contain primitive plants known as *Cyanobacteria* and *Prochloron* which play a similar role.

The giant clams farm zooxanthellae in their fleshy mantles, which they bathe in the sun during the day. The spectacular blue, green and brown colours of the mantles are in fact due to the zooxanthellae within, while tiny 'eyes' scattered in the mantle concentrate light to boost the production of the zooxanthellae.

Photosynthetically produced carbohydrates leak from the zooxanthellae into the clam's tissues, while special blood cells also harvest zooxanthellae and take them away to be digested. While all other bivalve species feed by filtering plankton from water, the giant clams obtain almost all their nutritional requirements from the zooxanthellae and can grow even in filtered sea water.

Recent work at James Cook University in Townsville has shown that giant clams, *Tridacna gigas*, grow very quickly, about 10 cm per year, and reach about 60 cm in ten years. Some reefs on the Great Barrier Reef have been overharvested by illegal Taiwanese fishermen, and clams have become scarce or even locally extinct

ABOVE: *Clams being grown in an experimental tank on Orpheus Island, site of the research station operated by James Cook University of North Queensland.*

because of fishing pressure in the Pacific Islands. Techniques have been developed to produce juvenile clams to reseed depleted reefs.

Clams are also used for aquaculture, for which they are ideal. They are easily raised in nurseries, are fast-growing, can be raised intertidally, and do not have to be fed.

The plant–animal partnerships have had amazing effects: huge clams weighing hundreds of kilograms which do not need to eat; and undersea mountains kilometres high created by blobs of jelly.

40

Unusual Partnerships

It is hardly surprising that many associations have developed among neighbours in the crowded coral reef ecosystem. A vast number of different species of plants and animals live in such close proximity that almost every tiny space is occupied by coral, sponges, sea squirts or other fast-growing colonial animals. The abundant hard shells and skeletons of many reef inhabitants create shelter for other vulnerable species; the food of animals, their wastes and mucus are stolen by others; and others may actually feed on the living tissue of their host, so that the association harms the host. Sometimes both partners benefit and neither can survive without the other.

Other relationships with branching corals

1. *Scale worm*
2. *Coral barnacle* — Cantellius *sp*
3. *Snail* — Coralliophila *sp.*
4. *Date mussel* — Lithophaga *sp*
5. *Serpulid worm*
6. *Gall crab* — Hapalocarcinus marsupialis
7. *Shrimp* — Periclimenes *sp.*
8. *Crab* — Cymo andreossyi
9. *Boring sponge* — Cliona

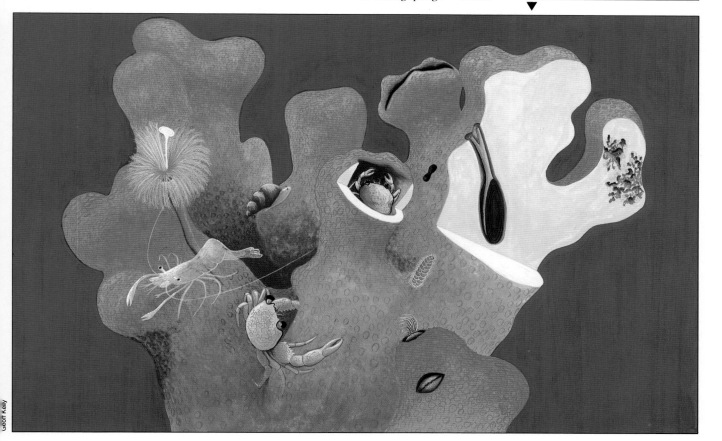

Geoff Kelly

BELOW: *A mess mate or pearlfish,* Onuxodon, *and a shrimp,* Anchistus, *live in a large-winged pearl oyster,* Magnavicula. *The fish may leave at night to hunt, but the shrimp remains inside feeding on material trapped on the oyster's gills.*

Coral — fish relationships

1. *Wrasse* — Thalassoma lunare
2. *Unicorn fish* — Oxymonacanthus longirostris
3. *Butterfly fish* — Chaetodon citrinellus
4. *Bird wrasse* — Gomphosus varius
5. *Humbug fish* — Dascyllus aruanus
6. *Puller fish* — Chromis caerulea
7. *Long-nosed butterfly fish* — Forcipiger longirostris
8. *Butterfly fish* — Chaetodon trifascialis
9. *Cardinal fish* — Apogon *sp.*
10. *Barramundi cod* — Cromileptes altivelis

L. Zann

41

4 ALL CREATURES GREAT AND SMALL

Coral reefs are home to an amazing array of animals, from tiny humbugs to giant gropers and sharks. In fact, the Great Barrier Reef has more species of fish than any other sea habitat.

While the brightly coloured corals and fish steal the limelight there are many other intriguing creatures, such as sea horses, spider crabs and the grotesque stonefish that lives superbly camouflaged among the shadowy rocks and on the sand.

D. McKillop/G.B.R.M.P.A.

At first sight, the Great Barrier Reef seems utterly confusing in its variety of colour, shape and movement. Even a single glance such as this one shows many different species. Some of the more interesting animals are the less obvious.

TOP INSET: *The black spotted toadfish is also known as a puffer fish because of its habit of blowing itself up when disturbed. It must present a formidable appearance to possible predators in this state.*

BOTTOM INSET: *The spiral tube worm, or Christmas tree worm, Spirobranchus, uses its beautiful branching arms to sieve its food from the water. At the slightest disturbance it withdraws them into its tube. The tube starts as a secretion of the baby worm on the surface of a coral. As the coral grows around it, the Spirobranchus grows at the same rate so that the opening of its tube remains on the surface.*

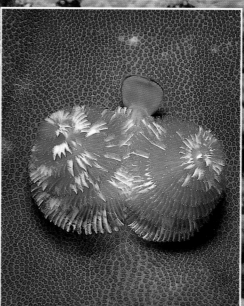

Animal Groups

Before taking a closer look at the incredible diversity of animal life on the Reef, it is useful to know a little bit about how animals have been organised into large groups (*phyla*) by scientists.

The main animal groups (*phyla*)	
Phylum Porifera	sponges
Phylum Coelenterata	corals and their relatives
Phylum Annelida	segmented worms
Phylum Crustacea	prawns, crabs and their relatives
Phylum Mollusca	seashells and their relatives
Phylum Echinodermata	sea-stars and their relatives
Phylum Chordata	a large group that includes sea squirts as well as vertebrates such as fish, birds, reptiles and mammals

Corals and Their Relatives

Corals belong to a large group of colourful and fascinating animals called the Coelenterata, or Cnidaria. As well as such well-known creatures as jellyfish, sea anemones and corals, the group includes the lesser known sea fans, sea pens and the fragile fern-like hydroids. Although coelenterates show a wide range of shapes and sizes, they share the same basic body plan — a simple sack-like stomach with a single mouth opening surrounded by a ring of stinging tentacles. Apart from the basic structural similarities, one feature common to all coelenterates is the presence of special stinging capsules.

Prawns and Their Relatives

Prawns belong to a large and varied group of animals that includes the familiar shrimps, crabs, crayfish and barnacles as well as many smaller and less well-known animals. Called the Crustacea, it is probably the most successful and important group of marine animals in the world. The Crustacea, with over 30 000 species, is such a large and varied group that it is often hard to see how all the animals are related. However, all crustaceans have a body covered with a protective shell, a number of jointed legs, two pairs of antennae and sometimes a pair of nippers. The body is divided into three parts: a head, a middle region (thorax) and a tail region (abdomen). Often the head and thorax are joined together and covered by a single shell called a carapace.

Plankton is the drifting life of the oceans. Most planktonic animals are very small but extremely numerous and form a very important part of marine food webs. Copepods are small crustaceans. They are the most common planktonic animals and are probably the most numerous animal group in the world. Together with copepods other small crustaceans, such as ostracods or water fleas, combine to make this varied group a very important part of the animal plankton.

ABOVE: *All coelenterates have tentacles that carry stinging cells, nematocysts, with which they paralyse and kill their prey. The tentacles shown here are part of a sea anemone.*
BELOW: *Gorgonian corals, sometimes called sea fans, are often brilliant colours. They frequently provide a perching place for feather stars. This combination of animals is more common in deeper waters. Gorgonians do not have symbiotic algae and hence do not need sunlight for their growth. Feather stars are crinoid echinoderms — relatives of the sea stars.*

44

LEFT: *Shrimps are common in Barrier Reef waters but most of them are small, transparent and not easily seen. An exception is the banded coral shrimp which has developed a specialised feeding strategy. It cleans fish — often while they sleep since it is usually active at night. It removes mucus, broken scales and small parasites.*

ABOVE: *Barnacles feed by sieving particles from the water. As larvae they are free living but settle down before they develop their adult shape and spend most of their lives attached, often to something floating. Shown here is one of the species of goose barnacle, so called because of its neck.*

BELOW: *Belying their name, hermit crabs are bold and easily seen. Sometimes a pool has more shells containing hermit crabs than shells containing their real builders!*

Seashells and Their Relatives

Coral reef shells show a delightful and almost endless array of shapes, colours and patterns. They belong to an animal group called the Mollusca. With over 75 000 members it is the second largest animal group in the world. Sea snails and their many relatives, including sea slugs, bivalves, chitons and squid, show an incredible range of shapes and forms. However, they all share the same basic body plan — a head, and a body supported on a singular muscular 'foot' (so called because it is generally used for movement). Many molluscs protect their bodies with some form of hard outer shell.

BELOW: *Its colouring and the way it swings its 'skirts' have given this nudibranch species,* Hexabranchus sanguineus, *the common name of Spanish dancer. Like other molluscs it usually creeps along on its foot but can swim like this when disturbed.*

N. Collins/G.B.R.M.P.A.

BELOW: *Most single-shelled molluscs have a door, an operculum, to close the shell opening. The spider shell, Lambis lambis, does not use its operculum like this. Instead it is claw shaped and used for digging and defence.*
BOTTOM: *Although cuttlefish do not look like molluscs, they do have a shell but it is completely internal.*

BELOW: *One of the cowrie shells, Cypraea. In cowries part of the body, the mantle, covers the outside of the shell when they are active. This keeps the shell free of encrusting creatures and is why cowrie shells found on the beach are usually so shiny.*

Sea Stars and Their Relatives

Sea stars (starfish) are common coral reef animals known as echinoderms. In many ways echinoderms are among the strangest of invertebrate animals. They have no real head or tail end. Instead their bodies are built on a radial pattern, often in a form with five sides. The name echinoderm, meaning spiny skin, relates to their outer surface which is covered with limestone plates that are often formed into spines.

All echinoderms are marine animals. Their most interesting feature is an amazing water-vascular system. This is a system of water-filled tubes ending in numerous finger-like projections that stick out through the skin. Known as tube feet, they often have suckers on the end and are used for movement. The water-vascular system works on water pressure, creating a network of tube feet that looks like hundreds of tiny, hydraulically operated legs.

ABOVE: *The sea urchins are one major group of the echinoderms and the one in which spines are best developed. Between the spines of this sea urchin can be seen its tube feet. The feet are attached to the animal's water vascular system. The tube feet operate on hydraulic principles and allow the urchin to move about, albeit rather slowly. The limestone plates on their surface have fused to form a continuous shell called a test. Urchins are grazers, scraping algae off the surfaces of rocks with their five jaws.*

48

BELOW: *The holothurians or sea cucumbers live in sandy and muddy areas. This cucumber has ejected sticky threads to distract and annoy a predator. The holothurians were once the basis for an important international fishery. Macassans from the island now called Sulawesi, used to come to northern Australia to collect them. After processing, they would be sold as bêches-de-mer.*

RIGHT: *Sea stars are probably the best known family of echinoderms. The tube feet are not obvious because they are limited to grooves on the underside of the animal.*

BOTTOM: *Brittle stars, ophiurians, have longer arms than sea stars. The arms are flexible and used for swimming. Brittle stars do not rely on tube feet for movement and are the fastest moving of the echinoderms.*

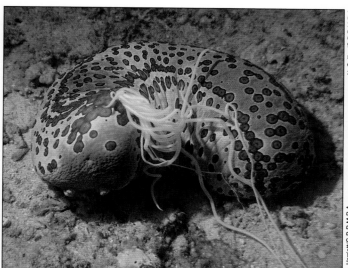

ABOVE: *The feather stars, or crinoids, are among the most beautiful of Reef creatures. The arms are very much divided compared with the sea stars. Crinoids do not move around very much but find a position where currents bring small animals to catch in the net of their arms.*

50

Sea Squirts

Sea squirts get their name from their feeding habits. They have two openings, called siphons, in their barrel-like bodies. Sea water is drawn in one siphon and then passed through the gut. Small food particles are filtered from the water which is then passed out through the other siphon. Sea squirts usually produce tadpole-like young (larvae). After a short free-swimming existence they settle to form new adults. The sessile (fixed) adults may live as a single animal or, in some types, may form colonies. There are many types of sea squirts to be found on the Reef, some being quite colourful.

TOP RIGHT: *Sea squirts are the solitary members of the group called ascidians. This solitary sea squirt, Phallusia julinea, clearly shows the two siphons which are its water circulation mechanism.*
RIGHT: *Although many sea squirts are inconspicuous, some are brilliantly coloured. It is difficult to believe, looking at these sedentary adults, that larval ascidians are very active and in some ways resemble vertebrates.*
BELOW: *This is one of the many ascidians that live in colonies. Sometimes the individuals are so closely connected they act as though they were a single animal. Other colonies are only connected in the loosest way.*

Peter Harrison/James Cook University

Ron & Valerie Taylor/A.N.T. Photo Library

Bryozoans

Bryozoans are minute animals that form coral-like colonies. Because many bryozoan colonies form hard, limestone skeletons they are often confused with corals. In fact zooids, the individual bryozoan animals, are much smaller and more complex than coral polyps.

Not all the zooids in a colony are the same. Some provide support for the colony. Others are designed for such tasks as feeding, cleaning and protecting the young. Bryozoan colonies show a wide range of forms and sizes varying from plant-like forms to flat sheets. Some, the so-called 'lace corals', look like small corals.

Bryozoans are often among the first animals to settle and grow on bare patches of the reef. As a result they may play an important part in cementing reefs. The limestone from their skeletons is also an important source of reef sediment.

Worms

Segmented marine worms (polychaetes) are members of the phylum Annelida. Earthworms are the most familiar animals in this group and they give a good idea of the general features of the group — a long, thin body divided into numerous segments. Some polychaetes are sedentary and live in tubes; others are mobile.

K. Atkinson/G.B.R.M.P.A.

TOP: *The so-called lace corals, really colonies of bryozoans, lift themselves above the surface on which they are growing, reducing the chance of being overgrown or smothered by sediment. Other bryozoans grow on bare rocks where there is less competition from other species.*

ABOVE: *This species of polychaete usually lives in a tube. Its tentacles are stretched over the surface of the bottom and used to catch particles of food.*

Sponges

Sponges are common and often colourful reef animals belonging to the phylum Porifera. They are often confused with plants because their simple bodies can take on almost any shape. Some are simple vase-like or tube-like growths. Others may form colourful crusts over rubble or dead coral. They also form growths that look like hands, fans or shrubs.

Whatever their shape, all sponges are built on the same lines — a hollow structure with a body wall built around a skeleton made of thousands of minute limestone or glassy structures called spicules. The outer wall of a sponge has many small holes (pores) through which water is drawn by the living cells inside. These cells feed by trapping minute food particles as they are carried past by the water. The water then passes out through larger holes in the body wall.

It is easy to see how early scientists saw sponges as plants rather than animals. Their simple bodies are like individual cells living as a colony, rather than a single animal made of many different types of cells.

TOP LEFT: *Sponges do not have skeletons but many have spicules or fibres buried in their walls. These make the sponge stiff and allow it to take on upright and even branching shapes. The spicules are often distinctive and are useful in identifying species of sponges. They are also a component of coral reef sand and make a contribution to consolidating coral reefs.*
TOP RIGHT: *A tiny flatworm can be seen crawling among the pores on the surface of a sponge. Each pore pulls water into the sponge so that food particles can be extracted from it.*
LEFT: *The central outward vents can easily be seen in this group of small sponges. The single coral polyp at the lower right gives an indication of scale.*

53

Reef Fish

Many people are content to explore the surface of the reef at low tide. To explore a little further, all that one needs is a face mask and snorkel or perhaps a glass-bottomed boat. Below the surface the reef explorer can come face to face with a world that is alive with the movement and colour of almost countless reef fish.

Scientists have recorded over 1500 types of fish on the Great Barrier Reef. Australian Museum workers found some 860 different types on a single reef. Many complicated factors have contributed to the vast numbers of different organisms, including fish, that inhabit the Reef. In simple terms, though, it can be said that the reef provides both a plentiful food supply and a great range of sheltering places.

The fish of the Reef have a wide range of feeding habits — plant-eating surgeon fishes, scavenging sweetlips and emperors, butterfly fish that feed on small invertebrates among the coral, parrotfish that scrape and bite coral and seaweed off dead corals, predatory coral trout and sharks, and many more.

Perhaps the most impressive feature of the Reef's fish life is the striking colour of the many smaller fish. In a few cases these colours may be a warning to predators that the fish are poisonous. In most cases, however, this is not so. In other marine communities such brightly coloured fish would be picked off easily by predators. In contrast, the Reef's many and varied coral structures provide a vast number of sheltering places for these weirdly camouflaged small fish.

Ron & Valerie Taylor/A.N.T. Photo Library

TOP: *Hand feeding fish is an experience that attracts divers to the Reef. The fish enjoying attention here are six-banded sergeant majors, Abudefduf.*
ABOVE: *The potato cod, Epinephalus tukutu, is one of the many species of cod found in the Reef region. The Cormorant Pass Section of the Great Barrier Reef Marine Park was declared specifically to protect this species but is now absorbed within the much larger Cairns Section.*

OPPOSITE: *The sweetlips are a popular group of Reef fish both for their colour and their distinctive flavour.*
TOP LEFT: *The butterfly fish are the quintessential coral reef fish — brightly coloured and numerous*
TOP RIGHT: *The coral cod is a member of the family Serranidae which also includes gropers and coral trout. Usually solitary, predatory fish, they are much sought after for the table.*

54

LEFT: *The brown booby, Suta leucogaster, may forage hundreds of kilometres out to sea in search of fish and squids. An adult is shown here with a well-grown young bird.*

BOTTOM: *A characteristic stalking pose of the reef heron or eastern reef egret, Egretta sacra, in search of fish in a tidal pool. Reef herons nest in colonies but not all at the same time. There may be nests from July to January.*

OPPOSITE TOP: *Most terns have a mainly white plumage but the noddy terns are black or brown with a white crown. The common noddy, Anous stolidus, is very typical of Great Barrier Reef cays and may occur in huge numbers. It often nests in Pisonia trees, a characteristic plant of well-vegetated cays.*

BELOW: *This is the crested tern, Sterna bergii, which breeds in many parts of Australia and forms big nesting colonies on some Barrier Reef cays.*

Birds of the Cays

A human visitor to a coral cay often puts to flight large flocks of seabirds that wheel and dip overhead screeching out raucous alarm calls. Cays provide an ideal home for many birds, especially sea birds. The seas of the reef abound with food and the islands provide relatively safe nesting grounds. Although many types of birds visit, live or nest on cays, a few are very common and well known.

On the reef flats at low tide, reef herons are often seen stalking their prey of small fish, crustaceans and molluscs. It is interesting to compare the numbers of the common white variety with the rarer slate-grey variety.

Terns are perhaps the most numerous of the sea birds found on cays; at least six or seven types are commonly seen. These birds are often found nesting, sometimes in their thousands, on the many sandy Reef islands. The white-capped noddy also nests on the sand but it prefers to build nests in the Pisonia trees.

Other sea birds that are commonly seen around coral cays are gulls, boobies, shearwaters, frigatebirds and gannets.

Two common ground birds that live in the forests on cays are the banded landrail and the bar-shouldered dove. Instead of depending on the sea for food, these birds rely on the island forests for their livelihood.

L. Zell/G.B.R.M.P.A.

M. Prociv/A.N.T. Photo Library

Marine Reptiles and Mammals

Reptiles and mammals generally live on the land. A few, however, have made their homes in the sea. Although marine reptiles and mammals are beautifully suited to their life in the sea, they must all return to the surface at regular intervals to breathe. Some, such as sea turtles and seals, must also return to the land to breed. Others, including whales, dolphins and sea snakes, are completely free of the land. They give birth to live young in the sea.

The tropical waters of the Great Barrier Reef region provide an ideal habitat for two types of marine reptiles — sea turtles and sea snakes. Sea turtles are commonly seen in some Reef waters. They nest on many Reef islands and some parts of the coast. Although less frequently seen, sea snakes are also quite common in some Reef waters.

Sea Snakes

About 15 types of sea snake occur in Great Barrier Reef waters. The olive sea snake (*Aipysurus laevis*) is one type most commonly encountered by divers. Like all sea snakes it has a flattened tail and is an excellent swimmer. It also avoids the problem of having to move onto land to breed by giving birth to live young in the sea. All sea snakes have very lethal venom but they have small fangs and are not normally aggressive animals. Having few natural enemies they are often inquisitive and will swim close to divers. Although there have been no reports of deaths from sea snake bites in the Great Barrier Reef region, all sea snakes should be treated with great respect.

Sea Turtles

Of the seven types of sea turtles found in the tropical waters of the world, six occur in Australian waters and three are common in Great Barrier Reef waters. By far the most commonly seen, both at sea and on shore, is the green turtle, *Chelonia mydas*. Mainly a plant eater, grazing on seaweeds and seagrasses, this large turtle may reach a weight of 180 kilograms.

Found in the tropical waters of the Atlantic, Pacific and Indian Oceans, the green turtle is well known for its tasty flesh. In the past, great numbers of green turtles and other sea turtles have been killed for food and soup. This was once such a large industry that there were even turtle soup canneries on Reef islands such as Heron Island. Although sea turtles are now protected in the Great Barrier Reef Marine Park, they are still killed for food, legally, by Aborigines and Torres Strait Islanders and, illegally, by poachers.

Other sea turtles common on the Reef are the large loggerhead turtle (*Caretta caretta*) and the smaller hawksbill turtle (*Eretmochelys imbricata*). Rare and endangered turtles, such as the huge leathery turtle (*Dermochyles coriacea*), have been seen in Reef waters and may even breed on some Reef islands or mainland beaches. For all sea turtles human activities provide a number of serious threats. Although these giant reptiles are now protected from hunters, their nesting islands must also be preserved.

BELOW: *Sea snakes are almost never dangerous in the water, even if their occasional friendliness can be an embarrassment, but if pulled up in a net or on a line they can be aggressive and difficult to handle.*

J. Oliver/G.B.R.M.P.A.

TOP: *The green turtle,* Chelonia mydas, *nests on a number of Barrier Reef islands and can sometimes be seen in Reef waters outside the breeding season.*
ABOVE: *The only marine herbivorous mammal, the dugong can be found in quiet bays and offshore areas where the water is shallow and warm. These conditions favour the growth of seagrasses on which the animal feeds.*

All sea turtles must return to land to lay their eggs. Green turtles and loggerhead turtles nest on many sandy Great Barrier Reef islands. On moonlit nights the large female turtles lumber up the beach and each digs a shallow pit above the high water mark. When the pit is deep enough the eggs are laid, up to 100 at a time. Before moving back to the sea the turtles cover the eggs with sand. The eggs hatch 6–12 weeks later.

Although marine mammals are more common in the Great Barrier Reef region than in many other parts of the world, they are less common than reef reptiles. Friendly dolphins may occasionally be seen, especially when they choose to swim alongside boats. Far more secretive are the dugongs or sea cows.

Dugongs

For centuries sailors have believed in half-human, half-fish creatures which lead ships to their doom on treacherous reefs. Lately, some writers have suggested that the rare marine mammal, the dugong, is responsible for these legends of 'mermaids'. Being mammals, the female dugongs feed their babies on milk from nipples near the base of their flippers. On a moonlit night, a dugong rising from the sea clasping her baby could look rather like a human mother. Dugongs are found in shallow tropical waters. They have bulky whale-like bodies up to three metres long and generally move sluggishly. Also called sea cows, dugongs feed on sea-grasses, which often grow like grassy meadows on the sea floor.

59

The Reef Nasties

Many Reef animals are venomous, poisonous or have sharp teeth or spines to deter predators or to kill their prey. The animals dangerous to humans — giant saltwater crocodiles and sharks, sea snakes, stonefish, fire corals, highly venomous seashells and many others should be treated with caution, and if common sense is used the risks are minimal.

Sharks

The dangers from sharks are legendary. Commonly seen on reefs, the small white tip (*Trianodon obesus*) and black tip (*Carcharhinus melanopterus*) reef sharks might look fearsome under water and have a mouthful of sharp teeth, but they are not dangerous if left alone. The rather aggressive small grey reef whaler (*Carcharhinus menisorrah*) has terrified many a Barrier Reef diver and, like the large, less common tiger sharks and hammerheads, should be treated warily. Giant gropers and large barracuda also have a bad reputation.

A few precautions will reduce risk of attack. Do not provoke any shark by swimming at dusk or when there is blood in the water. Don't panic. Always dive with a friend.

RIGHT: *The stonefish lives on muddy, stony bottom areas and is very difficult to see in its natural habitat. Its venom causes extreme pain.*
BELOW: *The gray reef whaler may be described as small but can seem quite big if you meet it underwater!*

Spiny and Venomous Fish

Many bony fish have protective spines and minor injuries are common among anglers. The aptly named surgeonfish (*Acanthurus*) have very sharp 'blades' at the base of their tails, while the rabbitfish (*Siganus*) have venomous spines capable of delivering a severe sting. Fatalities have been reported from overseas. Even more dangerous are the well-camouflaged stonefish (*Synanceja synanceichthys*) which have strong, sharp dorsal spines and a potent venom.

The various stingrays have sharp, knife-like serrated spines at the base of their long tails, grooved for the release of venom into the wound.

Sensible precautions reduce the risk of injury; wear thick-soled boots while reef walking; make sufficient noise to alert sleeping rays so they can move away; handle captured fish with care.

Bay Picture Library

LEFT: *This is the black surgeon fish,* Acanthurus achilles, *named for the surgeon's sharp scalpel. Its spine can be seen at the narrowest part of the tail, just where a predator's mouth or hand might grasp.*

BELOW: *The butterfly cod or fire fish,* Pterois antennata, *can inflict a very painful injury with its spines. It uses them to shepherd small fish into convenient corners where they can be grabbed. The prey fish do not realise what is happening to them until escape is impossible.*

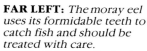

FAR LEFT: *The moray eel uses its formidable teeth to catch fish and should be treated with care.*
LEFT: Chironex fleckeri, *variously known as stinger, sea wasp or box jellyfish, is one of the most dangerous animals on the Reef. It is almost invisible in the water and its tentacles are very long.*
BELOW: *This scribbled toad fish,* Arothron mappa, *is poisonous to eat, as are most of its relatives in the family Tetradontidae.*
INSET: *All members of the coelenterate groups have stinging cells with which they kill their food. This stinging hydroid can inflict a very painful sting if it touches your skin.*

Stingers

During the hot summer months bathing along the tropical Queensland mainland is extremely hazardous. The deadly box jellyfish (*Chironex fleckeri*) is the most venomous marine animal known and is responsible for scores of deaths in Australia's tropics. The polyp stage lives in estuaries in winter while the medusa (jellyfish) stage emerges in early summer and remains relatively close to shore.

The risk is minimised by swimming in stinger-resistant enclosures and wearing protective clothing between October and April, but you are completely safe only if you stay out of the water.

First aid: bathe stings with vinegar; use cardiac massage and mouth-to-mouth resuscitation if heart and breathing stops.

Smaller box-jelly species (*Chiropsalmus*) extend offshore but are not a major risk for reef divers.

Reef Fire Corals and Anemones

A brush with fire coral (Millepora) or stinging hydroids (Aglaophenia, Lytocarpus) may result in a mild to rather severe sting with persisting rashes and itching. Some of the giant sea anemones (Stoichactis, Anthothoe) are also capable of inflicting very painful stings.

Prevention is best: do not touch; wear protective clothing.

Cone Shells

Among the most beautiful creatures in the sea, the spectacular cone shells (family Conidae) are capable of stinging the unwary shell collector. The cone-shell animal normally feeds by firing a minute harpoon into its prey, a worm, another snail or fish. A potent venom is injected, immobilising the prey. The fish feeders (*Conus geographus; C. tulipa*), recognised by their bulbous shells, are particularly venomous to man and there have been deaths in Reef waters. Stings are easily avoided: never pick up a cone shell.

Some Poisonous Reef Fish and Invertebrates

The inexperienced must be cautious about what they eat from the reef as many delicious looking fish and crabs can be poisonous.

Ciguatera, or fish poisoning, is a major problem in some parts of the tropics. Originating in a microscopic plant (*Gambierdiscus toxicus*) which lives attached to seaweeds, the poison ciguatoxin is ingested by herbivorous fish and concentrated by carnivorous fish in the food chain, and man. The potent toxin affects the nervous system. Symptoms range from nausea, skin tingles, numbness, cramps and skin rashes to coma and death in extreme cases.

Moray eels, large barracuda, certain rock cod (Serranidae) and snappers (Lutjanidae), and even Spanish mackerel from certain waters may be ciguatoxic at times on the Great Barrier Reef. Red bass (*Lutjanus bohar*) and chinamanfish are never eaten in these waters.

Precautions: seek local advice on the fish you catch; avoid eating large reef fish; if in doubt, don't.

The pufferfish, toadfish and porcupinefish (Tetraodontiformes) concentrate a potent toxin in their gonads, livers and intestines. They are extremely poisonous; Captain Cook nearly died after eating one of these fish in New Caledonia. In Japan, where the puffers are regarded as great delicacies, special restaurants are licensed to prepare pufferfish (Fugu). Despite this, there are numerous fatalities each year.

Spiny Problems — Crown-of-thorns Starfish and Sea Urchins

The infamous coral-eating starfish (*Acanthaster planci*) is also capable of inflicting a painful wound with its sharp spines, thought to be coated with a venomous mucus. The long-spined sea urchins (Diadema) may be a problem on fringing reefs where they are sometimes abundant; the thin spines can penetrate deeply into the skin and break off. Some urchins (e.g. Toxopneustes) have venomous pedicellariae, small pincers among their short spines, capable of inflicting a fatal sting.

5 IN DAYS GONE BY

Captain James Cook and Matthew Flinders made the first navigational maps of the Reef, as well as being the first to record the unique features found there.

Many other records about past events on the Reef are buried in the deep. The sometimes hazardous Reef waters are a grave-yard for many ships. Exploring old shipwrecks is a popular activity for divers today.

Kev Deacon/Dive 2000

The wreck of the Yongala has become a renowned dive site. Wrecks are natural experiments, showing how much coral growth can occur over a known period of time and how much marine life can be attracted to a previously barren area.

ABOVE INSET: One of the earliest wrecks on the Reef was James Cook's ship the 'Endeavour'.

BOTTOM INSET: Diving on a wreck site is an exciting way to learn history.

LEFT: *Aboriginal people have collected their food from waters of the Reef for centuries. Here a boy's fishing spear, used for catching fish in the shallows, is being made. Traditional Aboriginal fishing and hunting are permitted under carefully monitored conditions in the Marine Park.*
RIGHT: *Captain James Cook is renowned for his skill as a navigator. His logs, charts and sketches are models of their kind. He had a very good record for bringing his crews safely home. His attention to detail saved his expeditions on several occasions, not least in the difficult passage through the Great Barrier Reef.*

G.B.R.M.P.A.

National Library of Australia

Aborigines — the First Reef Explorers

The Great Barrier Reef was being explored by Aborigines over 15 000 years ago, before the development of the present form of the Reef.

Aboriginal groups operated from the beachfront and estuarine margins out to the sandbars, offshore islands and fringing reef systems. They possessed large outrigger canoes with single and double outriggers, which were capable of holding up to four adults. These canoes were paddled and used as hunting platforms as well as a means of transport.

Usually, these beach people lived within a small territory throughout the year and moved camp little more than half a kilometre at a time. Such shifts were nearly always to establish a clean campsite or to harvest a seasonal abundance of food, such as yams or crabs. Large gatherings were held at intervals of two to three years at well-established sites to carry out ceremonial activities.

Today, people living in Aboriginal communities in the Great Barrier Reef area (Palm Island, Wujal Wujal, Hopevale, Cooktown and Lockhart River) still use the marine and near shore resources which have played such an important role in the Aboriginal economy over the past several thousand years.

Early European Exploration

Evidence of exploration and exploitation of the Great Barrier Reef other than by Australian Aborigines is fragmentary prior to the voyage of exploration by James Cook in 1770. Chinese, Portuguese and Spanish mariners are known to have explored Timor and other areas to the north of Australia in the fifteenth and sixteenth centuries. Possibly such exploration extended to Australia. French maps of the mid-sixteenth century can be interpreted as delineating the north and east coasts of Australia. Those maps may have drawn on information collected in a Portuguese voyage of 1522–24 led by Torres Cristavao de Mendonca.

Captain Cook

Captain James Cook and the *Endeavour*

Captain James Cook, perhaps the best known of all British explorers, demonstrated remarkable skill and persistence to confirm the existence of the Great Southern Continent. The discoveries made by Cook during 1770, including his effort to chart a safe route along Australia's north-eastern coastline, constitute the beginning of the written records and modern use of the Great Barrier Reef.

The Cook Expedition was officially sent to make astronomical observations from Tahiti of the transit of Venus across the face of the sun. Cook was then to investigate and take possession of the Great Southern Continent whose existence had been postulated by geographers on the evidence of land sighting by other navigators. After circumnavigating New Zealand, Cook chose to sail west and locate the unknown east coast of 'New Holland'. He set a course for Van Diemen's Land, later known as Tasmania, at the point recorded by Abel Tasman's earlier voyage of 1642. Cook was driven north by storms and first sighted the mainland at Point Hicks. He then sailed north to examine and chart the east coast of Australia.

The first hazards that concerned Cook were the increasingly prolific shoals encountered from Bustard Bay, particularly in the area around Great Keppel Island. Proceeding cautiously northward through the Whitsunday Passage Cook passed Magnetic Island, believing that it affected his compass, and continued on to Green Island. This island was described by Joseph Banks as 'a small sand island laying upon a large coral shoal', and was the first of its kind so far sighted.

Unknowingly, Cook had already sailed over 1000 kilometres inside the Great Barrier Reef. Purposely sailing close to the mainland, he neither saw nor suspected a coral labyrinth to seaward. He continued his practice of night sailing until he reached Cape Tribulation, the point where his troubles began.

66

A Close Encounter with the Reef

Despite 'heaving the lead' continuously to check water depth, the *Endeavour* 'struck and stuck fast' on a small coral reef not far from Cape Tribulation. Fortunately, expert seamanship, continuous pumping and some jettisoning saved the ship. Yards and top masts were struck and everything done to lighten the ship. The six ten-pounder guns were thrown overboard followed by a large quantity of iron and stone ballast from the hold.

Cook then took a gamble and put as many men as could be spared from the pumps to man the longboats and tow the *Endeavour* free. A sail, covered with oakum and other rubbish that would stop the leak, was hauled under the ship's bottom until the inward rushing water pressed it against the hull. With the two longboats scouting the way, Cook nosed the *Endeavour* cautiously up the coast, passing two islands which he called Hope Islands.

On the way, a bay that proved too shallow for the ship was named Weary Bay out of sympathy for the tired rowers. After four days searching for a safe harbour to repair damages, Cook finally edged into the mouth of the Endeavour River where Cooktown now lies. The ship remained there for two months while repairs were carried out.

Deciding to risk the dangers of the maze of reefs, Cook then attempted to sail to the open sea but soon found himself bound in by long ribbon reefs. He turned north, attempting to 'get in with the land again', but was again confronted by seemingly impenetrable reefs. The *Endeavour* headed for a rocky island inhabited by large monitor lizards, which he named Lizard Island. Cook and Joseph Banks, the expedition's botanist, climbed to its highest point to look for a safe passage. From here 'breaks or partitions' could be seen in the reefs, with sufficient deep water for the *Endeavour* to pass safely.

TOP: *Magnetic Island was named by Cook, who wrongly blamed it for problems with his compass. This shot shows Radical Bay on the north-east of the island.*
ABOVE: *Lizard Island also owes its name to Cook who was impressed by the numerous goannas there. Modern visitors to the island are equally impressed by their descendants.*
BELOW: *James Cook was born in the town of Whitby in north-eastern England. The house where he was born has been rebuilt in the Treasury Gardens in Melbourne.*

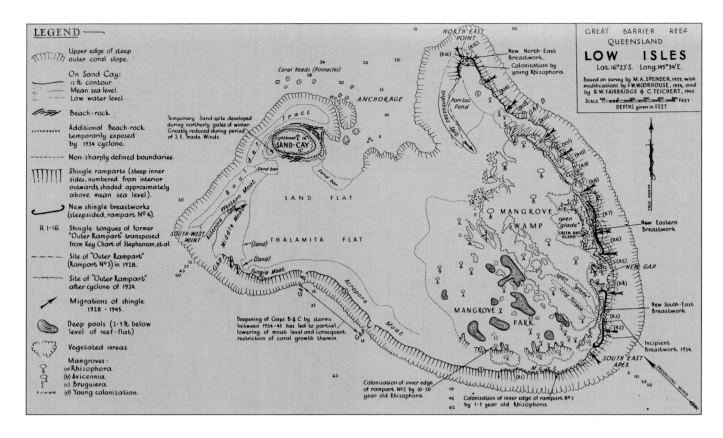

GREAT BARRIER REEF QUEENSLAND
LOW ISLES
Lat. 16°23'S. Long. 145°34'E.

Based on survey by M.A. SPENDER, 1929, with modifications by F.W. MOORHOUSE, 1934, and by R.W. FAIRBRIDGE & C. TEICHERT, 1945.

Using a longboat and sounding to confirm clear passage, Cook resolved 'to quit the coast altogether' Open sea was gained through a break in the ribbon reefs known as Cook's Passage. Having reached the sea he then proceeded north.

The open sea, however, presented a new peril. With no winds to control direction the *Endeavour* was being forced back towards the Great Barrier Reef. Anchorage was impossible because of the extreme depth. In an effort to counter the relentless surge, the *Endeavour*'s longboats were again deployed to tow the vessel north. Miraculously, a mere 80 metres from certain destruction a light wind caught the sails and moved the ship out of harm's way.

With the aid of a light breeze and a favourable tide, Cook passed through the tiny opening 'Providential Channel' to safety. Cook's relief is apparent from his journal. 'It is but a few days ago that I rejoiced at having got without the Reef but the joy was nothing compared to what I now feel at being safe at anchor within it.'

RIGHT: *Endeavour Reef looks beautiful on a clear day with a good view. It must have seemed very different to Cook and his men in a small ship in foggy weather with no chart or knowledge of the surrounding waters. One of the problems Cook faced was his unfamiliarity with Barrier Reef tidal heights and patterns. Used to the North Sea tides, which are usually twice a day and similar in height, he was not prepared for the semidiurnal Reef tides. He hoped the* Endeavour *would float free at the next high tide after she struck, and was dismayed when she stuck fast. He did not have enough local knowledge to consider the strategy of waiting for the high tide after that.*

Cook Claims the Coast for Britain

Advancing through Endeavour Strait, Cook reached the northernmost tip of Australia, which he named Cape York in honour of the Duke of York and confirmed Australia's separation from New Guinea. From a small rocky island known as Possession Island, Cook then took formal and ceremonial possession of the coast in the name of the Crown.

His splendid series of charts earned him the title 'founder of Australian hydrography', and laid the foundations for British colonisation. He located and christened nearly everything in sight including reefs, bays, isles, heads and capes, most of which still bear his names. With the help and expertise of Joseph Banks the expedition recorded invaluable scientific data on the Great Barrier Reef, and a steady stream of marine surveyors and scientists followed in Cook's footsteps.

Natural Images/A.N.T. Photo Library

68

From *A Voyage to Terra Australis*, Mathew Flinders; London, G. and W. Nicol, 1814. Facsimile Edition — the Adelaide Libraries Board of South Australia, 1966

LEFT: *Matthew Flinders was one of the finest chartmakers from the great British traditional school. He was only twenty-seven when, in 1801–02, he circumnavigated Australia in the* Investigator. *The Great Barrier Reef owes its name to him.*
ABOVE: *Flinders' soundings were still used on charts of the Great Barrier Reef region until very recently.*

Captain Matthew Flinders

On 18 July 1801, Captain Matthew Flinders and his crew sailed the *Investigator* from England, in a quest to explore the land and water north of Sydney. Early in 1802 the *Investigator* took port on the Victorian coast, where Flinders and his men investigated the surrounding territory for several weeks. After leaving Victoria the *Investigator* travelled south to reach Sydney on 8 May 1802.

The ship remained anchored in Sydney for two months before Flinders and his crew were prepared to return north for further explorations. On 22 July 1802, they left Sydney and scanned the north coast and part of the inner passage of the Great Barrier Reef until 18 October.

Captain Flinders is an often overlooked figure in Australian navigational history; his detailed explorations and precise mappings of coastal Australia and the Great Barrier Reef are still used as the basic charts of the Reef today.

Flinders Charts the Reef

From 22 July–18 October 1802, the *Investigator* travelled along the north coast and through part of the inner passage of the Great Barrier Reef in an attempt to explore the irregularities of the coast. From 5 to 11 October Flinders' boat was in turmoil as indicated by two entries in his journal.

7 October. The appearance of shoals were very numerous this morning, the shadows of white clouds, ripplings, and smooth places, being scarcely distinguishable from reefs. Our whaleboat, however, enabled us to discriminate, and in a little time I learned to disbelieve all appearances but those where something was above water, or where the water had a tinge of green in it; with all these deductions, however, there still remained a formidable mass of reefs, through which there appeared to be but one small channel.

8 October. The prospect at noon today is still worse than ever; for except to the westward, whence we came, the reefs encircle us all round . . . The breakers to the eastward denote the outside of these reefs to be exposed to the open sea, and are, indeed, the only alleviation to the hopelessness of our present prospect.

In R. Thynne's book, *Captain Flinders' Explorations and Adventures*, several more depictions of the Reef are recorded from Captain Flinders' journal. When first entering the passage Flinders describes it as a

. . . singular coral formation, though here nearly a hundred miles distant, and therefore invisible. As might be expected, this barrier acted as a breakwater, leaving the inner channel comparatively calm. However, it was a calmness by no means to be implicitly trusted; for to say nothing of its very unequal depths, and the numerous small islets, also of coral, with which it is interspersed, there are coral pillars or columns rising from the bottom, but not appearing on the surface, which would rip a vessel from stem to stern if come into collision with . . .

In an effort to manoeuvre the ship safely through the uncertainty of the Reef, small boats were sent ahead to scan the breadth and depth of water covering the everchanging structure of the Reef. One of the greatest risks they encountered was to sail the ship near the inner edge of the Barrier, where the water suddenly became shallow and the Reef appeared to be guarded by its own fortress of coral. While navigating the *Investigator* through the Reef, Flinders carefully mapped out a safe path which today is known as Flinders' Passage.

Captain Flinders' knowledge of botany and marine biology made him a reliable source for scientists. His perception of the Reef's coral structures was very up to date with what was known at that time when he wrote: 'These makers of coral are polyps, or masses of jelly, provided with a number of radiating arms, which draw in the surrounding water, thus supplying nutriment to the main body or mass.' He went on to describe the building process that corals perform to reach the multi-level bulk that is singularly called a reef.

ABOVE: *Flinders was understandably impressed by the clams he saw on the Great Barrier Reef. They have been heavily fished since then, both legally and illegally, so we probably no longer have clams in the size and number that Flinders saw. We can still be impressed by the size and colour of the younger specimens now rebuilding their populations under full protection.*

RIGHT: *Flinders compared coral growths such as these to gardens and flower arrangements. Fine areas of coral are often now referred to as coral gardens.*

70

From the fact of these little coral-makers being unable to prolong existence above high-water mark, the whole formation exhibited mainly, a floor or platform at that level. Here and there are a larger knob, about the size, and pretty nearly about the colour, of a negro's head, protruded above this main level. But these were 'dead coral'; that is to say, the makers had long ceased to exist and disappeared, and those portions of coral-rock had become discoloured by exposure to weather.

Inspecting a tidal pool, Flinders compared the marine life he observed to the products of a harvest field and a garden.

Here, underwater, appeared to be reproduced or imitated the products of the harvest field and the garden, but with glowing tints far in excess of the land. Wheat-sheaves, mushrooms, staghorns, cabbage-leaves, and a host of other imitative forms were quite as various as the forms themselves, and the several shades of green, purple, brown, and white were far more vivid than the florist's care and art had ever succeeded in producing.

Flinders wrote at great length about the tremendous clams dispersed about the floor of the Reef between the pillars of coral.

These cockles did not bury themselves in the sand as their puny English prototypes do, nor were they found attached to any stationary substance. They merely lay loosely on the rock, being covered with water at high tide, and dry during the ebb. During these latter periods they lay half-open, but closed with a loud bang on the approach of footsteps.

Concluding his account of the trip through the Reef, Flinders wrote that in his earliest years he had read of others' adventures in the Pacific Ocean, and had believed the water was true to its name — pacified and tranquil. Finding it otherwise during his own exploration, he wrote: 'I have never seen such elemental fury so impetuous as on this very coast, and that as well of wind as water.'

Survey and Exploration

Cook's voyage was one of scientific exploration, and the Great Barrier Reef has been the subject of many subsequent voyages and expeditions of survey and exploration. Following Cook and Flinders there was Ferdinand Bauer and Robert Brown in the *Cato* and *Porpoise* 1801–03; Phillip Parker King in the *Mermaid* and *Bathurst* 1819–21; Stokes, Wickham, Bynoe and others in the *Beagle* 1839–41; Blackwood, Jukes and MacGillivray in the *Fly* and the *Bramble* 1842–45; MacGillivray, Stanley and Huxley in the *Rattlesnake* 1847–49; Denham in the *Herald* 1853–61; Mosely and others in the *Challenger* 1874; Coppinger and Miers in the *Alert* 1881 and McFarlane in the *Constance* 1887. W. Saville-Kent, as the Commissioner for Fisheries to the Government of Queensland, systematically explored most parts of the Reef, and in 1893 published his historic book, *The Great Barrier Reef*, which includes the first photographs of the Reef's coral splendour.

More recent expeditions include that led by Charles Hedley of the Australian Museum to Masthead Island in 1904; the Royal Australian Ornithological Expedition to North West Island in 1910; the Royal Zoological Society of New South Wales Expedition to North West Island in 1925; the Great Barrier Reef Committee Expeditions in 1926 to Michaelmas Cay and in 1937 to Heron Island to sink geological bore holes; the Royal Society of London Expedition of 1928–29 led by C. M. Yonge, whose members spent a year on Low Isles in 1928–29; the 'Steers' Expedition which investigated the entire length of the Barrier Reef in 1937 and 1938; the 1954 Expedition which revisited Low Isles, and the Royal Society and Universities of Queensland Expedition of 1973 led by D. R. Stoddart.

BELOW: *The coral reef edge usually shows a good growth of corals and a variety of fish species.*

Wrecks of the Reef

In the early 1800s, the navigator Matthew Flinders first used the term 'Great Barrier Reef' which now describes the vast complex of reefs and islands off the Queensland coast, extending 2000 km from the Capricorn–Bunker coral cays to Torres Strait. From the early days of European colonisation, vessels have plied these reef waters on the trade routes to Asia and beyond and to harvest the region's resources.

Ships' captains had two main choices when sailing north. To sail within the outer reefs to Cape York gave some protection from the Pacific swells but required careful navigation. The alternative was to pass seaward of the barrier reefs to reach Torres Strait via the Great North-East Channel or via Raine Island Entrance and Blackwood Channel. Vessels wishing to traverse the Barrier Reef elsewhere had to risk passages through narrow gaps in the reefs. Sailing craft were particularly vulnerable to the vagaries of wind and currents, and to thread the maze of uncharted reefs required great skill and courage.

The hazards involved in navigating the labyrinth of reefs, compounded at times by strong tidal currents, storms and cyclones, resulted in the loss of many vessels, large and small. Some reef waters are ship graveyards. Around the reefs of the Capricorn–Bunker Group in the south lie the remains of numerous vessels. The reefs around Raine Island Entrance to the far north have also claimed many wrecks. A fierce cyclone which swept Bathurst and Princess Charlotte Bays in 1899 caused the loss of 300 lives and 59 vessels from the pearling fleet sheltering there.

Early Shipping

Recorded European navigation in Reef waters began with Captain Torres who, in 1606, sailed the Spanish caravel *San Pedrico* through the strait which now bears his name.

British exploration began with James Cook in the barque *Endeavour*. Cook's reports led to the founding of the colony of New South Wales. Within two decades extensive maritime surveys had begun to chart the way for the increasing numbers of vessels bringing convicts, immigrants and supplies to the new settlements and sailing north to Torres Strait on the homeward journey.

From the early days, enterprising colonists fitted out vessels to hunt whales. Other maritime industries and trades developed — bêche-de-mer fishing, sandalwood cutting, pearl-shell collecting and guano mining — in some cases leading to special designs such as the pearling lugger.

With the spread of settlement, a coastal trade network was established. By the 1850s, numerous small wooden sailing vessels — usually schooners and brigs — were competing for cargo and passengers.

During the 1860s, Queensland saw the establishment of a new trade called 'blackbirding' — the recruitment and transport of Pacific islanders to work on Queensland sugar plantations. A series of gold rushes in Queensland also led to many vessels entering these waters bringing fortune seekers, including European and Chinese, to newly established landings.

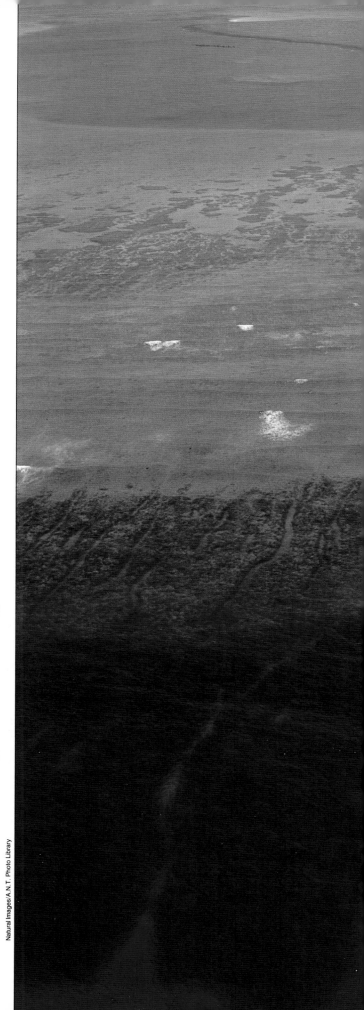

72

Ken Garnett

LEFT: *This aerial view shows the fate of the trawler* Pacific Lady *grounded during rough weather on Boult Reef in 1985.*
ABOVE: *Divers visit the relics of the* Yongala.
BOTTOM: *Many sailing ships were lost, or lost their gear in the Barrier Reef. This old anchor has become home to various encrusting crustacea and molluscs.*

Immigrants arriving in Australia in large numbers from the early 1840s were carried in specially fitted vessels. To increase profits, owners sought return cargoes. Exports included wool, wheat, sugar, coal, gold and timber. Passengers leaving Australia included detachments of military regiments.

The pageant of early exploration, settlement, development, trade and transport may be revealed by the remains of vessels lying broken up or relatively intact, encrusted in coral or partially buried in seabed sediment in Great Barrier Reef waters. The wrecks show technological developments in naval architecture and advances made in propulsion such as steam power and the internal combustion engine. Wreck sites represent a priceless irreplaceable heritage.

Ron & Valerie Taylor/A.N.T. Photo Library

73

Stories from the Deep

About 1200 shipwrecks before 1900 are on record. The earliest identifiable relics from the Great Barrier Reef are six cannon and other heavy objects jettisoned from the *Endeavour* in 1770 to refloat the vessel after it struck a reef. The cannon were recovered and restored for public display.

Morning Star (1813–1814): This Indian-built brig was wrecked near Temple Bay, far north Queensland, at a location yet to be pinpointed. The brig carried a general cargo of colonial exports and was bound for Batavia (now Jakarta). When located, its remains should generate new insights into Indian and European shipbuilding practices and techniques, and the trade relations Australia had with South-East Asia at the time.

HMS *Mermaid* (1816–1829): Few records exist for this type of vessel. This cutter was built of teak in Calcutta using European and Indian designs and construction techniques. The *Mermaid* was converted to a schooner for official survey and supply duties, and was commanded by Phillip Parker King in surveys of the Australian coast between 1818 and 1820. She was lost south of Trinity Inlet, Cairns.

America (1827–1831): Built in Quebec and used for convict transport, this ship arrived at Hobart in 1831 with 186 female convicts. She then sailed for Batavia but the southern reefs claimed her and she was abandoned on Wreck Island reef off Gladstone.

Golden City (1852–1865): First used for the California Gold Rush, this American-built clipper became an immigrant ship plying between England, Australia and New Zealand. She was wrecked at Lady Elliott Island while loading guano for export.

SS *Gothenburg* (1865–1875): Built in London as the SS *Celt*, the screw steamer was lengthened in 1866 and renamed *Gothenburg*. This iron vessel was also rigged as a three-masted schooner and on her last voyage was carrying general cargo and gold bullion from the Pine Creek diggings south of Palmerston (now Darwin). Among the 84 passengers were various dignitaries and miners who were carrying gold-laden money belts. The ship struck Old Reef off Ayr, drowning 106 people.

Queensland Museum

ABOVE: *Tobacco pipes and ceramic armbands — part of the property of Pacific islanders travelling on the* Foam *when she was wrecked in 1877.*

Foam (1873–1877): Wrecked on Myrmidon Reef off Townsville, this blackbirding schooner was returning Pacific islanders who had completed their indenture period on sugar plantations. All were saved. Systematic study of this vessel should contribute greatly to an interesting facet of Queensland's history. To date, trade objects raised and conserved include ceramic armlets, manufactured to imitate traditional ornaments carved from giant clam shells.

Yongala (1903–1911): This single-screw passenger steamer sank in a cyclone off Cape Bowling Green, south-east of Townsville, with the loss of all 120 on board and its general cargo. The wreck is lying on the seabed with the hull virtually intact, providing a valuable archaeological resource and a home for interesting marine life.

BELOW: *An artist's impression of the* SS Gothenberg *in the stormy seas that wrecked her in 1831.*

Queensland Museum

Ken Garnett

74

TOP LEFT: *Although the Yongala was wrecked in 1911, the site of the wreck remained a mystery until the 1970s. It lies in deep water quite close to the main shipping channel.*
ABOVE *and* **LEFT:** *The Yongala dive is considered difficult and only suitable for advanced divers. The combination of historical relics and exceptionally fine coral and marine life makes the dive an unforgettable experience.*
BELOW: *Built on the Wearside, the Yongala was considered a very well-appointed vessel. Her loss with all aboard was one of Australia's worst shipping disasters.*

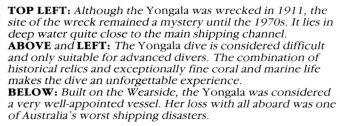

Visiting Wrecks Today

Most wrecks lie in the intertidal zone or below the tideline. Their value as a cultural resource includes not only their archaeological importance but also their attraction to divers. If relatively intact, they can host many reef fish and other marine life. Recognisable objects such as cannon, anchors, deck machinery, crockery and glassware add to the excitement of wreck diving.

These irreplaceable relics must be treated with great care. Anchoring directly over the site or the use of explosives to uncover artefacts causes great havoc. Even minor disturbances can begin a process of erosion and degradation in a wreck where the processes of disintegration have more or less stabilised. Removing relics also robs other divers of the chance to 'discover' them anew. Once removed from the water, relics deteriorate rapidly if not properly conserved.

Ben Cropp Productions

TOP: *Heavy objects such as cannons were sometimes discarded to lighten ships that were in trouble in rough weather. Many wrecks occurred in Barrier Reef waters that were not recorded or which have never been found. The source of this particular cannon is not known.*
RIGHT: *The anchor from the Ferguson, wrecked in 1840 on Ferguson Reef, dwarfs an exploring diver. Ferguson Reef is in the far north of the region where the Reef comes close to the mainland and finding a passage through the maze is very difficult.*
BELOW: *Wrecks may yield poignant mementos such as this regimental buckle from the Ferguson. Known wreck sites are given protective zoning by the Great Barrier Reef Marine Park Authority to ensure that they are not damaged. Some also receive protection under the Historic Shipwrecks Act.*

Ben Cropp Productions

Ben Cropp Productions

Preserving the Wrecks

All wreck sites and objects have some cultural value and their preservation will receive increasing attention in the future. Most sites will be left almost untouched; some may be partially or fully excavated with the objects conserved and samples displayed in museums and interpretation centres. Wreck-diving trails are planned for some key sites.

Practical training courses in wreck survey and related fields are run periodically by the Maritime Archaeological Association of Queensland. Programs include shipwreck assessment, artefact conservation and historical records research.

Shipwrecks and the Law

All shipwrecks and relics remain the property of their lawful owners or the Crown. The most relevant legislation is the Commonwealth's Navigation Act 1912 and the Historic Shipwrecks Act 1976. The former covers salvage laws and relates primarily to people who are in possession of salvaged material.

The 1976 Act and its regulations have the ultimate aim of protecting our maritime heritage by providing for the protection of historic shipwrecks and relics. Declared wrecks in the Great Barrier Reef region are the *Pandora*, *Morning Star, Mermaid, Gothenburg, Quetta, Foam* and *Yongala*. A reward may be paid to the discoverer if a previously unlocated wreck is declared historic.

Regulations apply to declared shipwrecks and relics to prohibit their disturbance or removal. Protected zones in Reef waters have been declared around the *Pandora, Yongala* and *Foam*. Under Queensland's Marine Parks Act 1982, all wrecks and relics within state marine parks are protected.

The Queensland Museum has a Maritime Archaeology branch which is actively collecting material from wrecks and caring for it. Wrecks provide a peephole into the past because everything associated with life on the ship remains fixed on the day it was lost.
TOP, TOP RIGHT and **RIGHT:** *Artefacts from HMS* Pandora *wrecked on Pandora Reef in 1791. She had been despatched to recapture the* Bounty *and its mutinous crew, four of whom were drowned in the wreck.*
BELOW: *The* Quetta *is one of the wrecks which has been declared under the Historic Shipwrecks Act.*

6 THE REEF AND US

Millions of visitors from all over the world come to see and admire the natural beauty of the Great Barrier Reef. The resources of the Reef have been used by humans for over 40 000 years, beginning with the Aborigines who hunted and fished in the region.

Early European settlers quickly made use of the plentiful food source and, as early as the mid-1800s, bêches-de-mer and trochus were harvested commercially. Guano (phosphate rock) was also mined in the region.

Today tourism and fishing are the major industries in the area. The diverse biology of the Reef also offers tremendous opportunities for research.

In 1975 the Great Barrier Reef was declared a Marine Park and the Marine Park Authority was set up to monitor Reef use and promote Reef conservation.

Management of the Marine Park emphasises protection of the environment for the wise use and enjoyment of this and future generations. The four-lined snapper, Lutjanus kamira, is only one of the many Barrier Reef fish which have come to accept the presence of divers.
INSET: The protected pools of a cay such as Heron Island are ideal places to become familiar with some of the many species of Reef animals.

Tourism

Tourism is the largest commercial activity in economic terms. In 1986–87 an estimated 700 000 people visited the Reef and in the process spent over $200 million.

For its huge size, there are remarkably few places to build resorts on the Great Barrier Reef. There are 24 island resorts along the Reef region coast. Resort guests make use of reefs and waters for recreational activities including fishing, diving and snorkelling, water sports, sightseeing, reef walking and some collecting.

The number of visitors to the Reef doubled from 1981 to 1985 and continues to increase. This increase is a result of improved technology, mainly the increasing use of high-speed catamarans which allows tourists to be transported to the Reef comfortably and quickly on day trips, and the use of reef-based constructions such as pontoons.

ABOVE: *Each day, high-speed catamarans transport tourists to pontoons, such as this one, which is moored at Norman Reef in the Cairns Section of the Marine Park. Pontoons operate under strict environmental controls and there are continuous monitoring programs to ensure that they do not cause any damage to the Reef*

BELOW: *Boats of every sort help tourists to enjoy the Reef. Trips may offer fishing, diving, snorkelling, reef walking or island visits. Day-trip charter vessels, such as this, allow small groups of visitors to take advantage of the experienced crew's knowledge of the Marine Park, its zoning plans and recreational activity areas.*

Fishing

In economic terms the fishing industry is second to tourism, being worth an estimated $150 million annually. Commercial fishing in the Great Barrier Reef region has expanded dramatically in the last 25 years. In 1965, for example, there were 50 trawlers working the area; by 1986 this number had increased to 1400. This large expansion was due mainly to the new-found export markets for Australian prawns and led to the prawn boom of the 1970s and 1980s. Today the fleet is restricted to 950 trawlers working the prawn and scallop grounds of the Reef region.

Trawling is not without its problems. In the early 1980s, over-capitalisation and too many boats trying to share a limited resource saw many trawler operators face financial hardship which forced them to leave the industry. The trawler fleet is now subject to careful control and management measures are being implemented to reduce effort.

While prawns and scallops provide the basis of the commercial fishing industry, there is also a market for fin fish such as coral trout, sweetlip, red emperor and mackerel. Although most of the prawns are destined for export markets the majority of the fin fish caught in Barrier Reef waters are for local consumption, either in Queensland or southern states.

Gillnet fishing is also important. Fishermen operate mainly in inshore waters catching the famous barramundi and northern salmon as well as numerous other estuary species. At certain times of the year they also catch substantial quantities of school mackerel along the coastal inshore areas.

Spanish Mackerel are caught by trolling near the reef in the last three months of each year and form the mainstay of the fish and chip shop trade in Queensland.

LEFT: *Commercial prawning is an important activity in the Barrier Reef region.*
RIGHT: *As well as prawns and fish, scallops are a valuable marine product in the region. The species fished in Queensland is the saucer scallop,* Amusium, *a different genus from the commercial catch in southern waters.*
BELOW: *Scallops must be removed from their shells — known as shucking — before they can be sold.*

Recreational Fishing

Recreational fishing is the largest participator sport in the world. It is estimated that some 1.2 million people annually 'wet a line' in Queensland.

Game fishing is without doubt the most glamorous type of recreational fishing. Mention game fishing to most people and they immediately think of giant marlin caught from large, expensive boats, a sport only for the wealthy. In recent years, however, many anglers have found they can catch a range of exciting game fish species, including billfish (marlin and sailfish), from the ordinary family powerboat.

Giant black marlin attract anglers from around the world. These giants of the underwater world gather each spring, from September to November, along the seaward edge of the Great Barrier Reef where the edge of the Reef lies along the continental shelf. This is the only known place in the world where such an aggregation occurs.

The fish range in size from youngsters of 50–60 kg, up to fish in excess of 600 kg. All the truly giant fish are females as the male black marlin grows only to a mere 200 kg. The largest black marlin caught in these waters to date weighed 655 kg.

Cairns is the home port to most of the marlin fleet and from that a huge tourism industry has developed.

The more numerous smaller black marlin abound in the food-rich waters of the inner Barrier Reef and the waters between the Reef and the mainland. These black marlin and the similar-sized sailfish are the primary species sought by the light tackle sport and game fishermen.

Just offshore from Townsville, in the Cape Bowling Green area, a natural phenomenon results in a large concentration of these smaller billfish members each year. Anglers fishing from professionally crewed charter vessels have caught up to 16 billfish in one day from the one boat.

Among the local population the most popular form of recreational fishing on the Reef is bottom fishing for species such as coral trout, sweetlip and red emperor. Bottom fishing on the Reef, which accounts for most of the fish caught on the Great Barrier Reef, is usually done with heavy handlines as opposed to rods and reels.

More fish are caught in the Great Barrier Reef area by recreational fishing than by commercial fishing, with both visitors and locals actively participating in the sport.
ABOVE: This red bass is regarded as non-edible because of the possibility of ciguatera toxin in its flesh.
RIGHT: Light tackle gamefishing pits the angler's skill against the cunning and instinct of the fish. Gamefishermen usually tag and release billfish.

82

Holidays on the Reef

The Great Barrier Reef is one of the biggest holiday places in Australia.

Recreation on the Reef means many things to many people. To the fisherman it is large, colourful, delicious fighting fish; to the reef watcher, scientist, walker, photographer, snorkeller or diver it is abundant, fascinating, curious life; to the boatman it is clear blue water, sunshine, exotic anchorages and swimming, reef watching and fishing at distant locations; to the camper it is tropical islands of white sands near blue lagoons, the chance to swim, sunbake or explore a fascinating world and maybe catch a fish for dinner.

Fishing has long been popular, and diving, which is relatively new, has shown a remarkable growth in the last five years. The Reef offers divers everything they could wish for. The novice diver can experience calm clear waters in lagoons filled with colourful corals and fish; for the more experienced there is the prospect of hanging suspended near a vertical wall of coral that drops off into an abyss, or exploring one of the many wrecks that lie along this well-known navigational hazard.

Spearfishing has long been a popular activity on the Reef, with its relatively shallow waters and the multitude of large colourful fish that make good targets as well as good eating.

With over 4000 species of molluscs on the Great Barrier Reef, most of which have beautiful, hard outer skeletons or shells, it is no wonder that shell collecting is so popular. There are many shell clubs in Queensland whose members are shell experts and own extensive shell collections.

Many people have gained inspiration from the Reef's tapestry of shapes and colours and its many moods, among them artists, poets, photographers and weavers.

TOP LEFT: *Being in the water with the teeming life of the Great Barrier Reef is an exhilarating experience. In Marine National Park areas, fish often lose their fear of divers and snorkelling provides an ideal opportunity to watch animals going about their normal lives.*
TOP RIGHT: *Safety precautions are important when snorkelling — always go snorkelling with a buddy and have a responsible person keeping a lookout.*
LEFT: *Underwater breathing apparatus gives the diver more freedom underwater but involves careful training and personal discipline. Many places along the Queensland coast offer training in diving and opportunities for the trained diver to explore the Reef.*

G.B.R.M.P.A.

ABOVE: *Research often starts with careful observation and collecting in the field.*
BELOW: *Low Isles was the site of the first major research project in the region. The Great Barrier Reef Expedition, 1928–30, under the leadership of C. Maurice Yonge, was funded partly by the British Association and partly by Australian bodies such as the Great Barrier Reef Committee. The object of the expedition was to collect Reef animals and study the geology and structure of the reefs and islands.*

Research on the Reef

The urge to know more about the Great Barrier Reef has driven naturalists and scientists to embark on more than a dozen major research expeditions.

More recently, four Great Barrier Reef scientific research stations have been built on Reef islands. These, and the development of major research facilities in coastal cities, have allowed scientists to carry out complex research on the spot.

As a number of complex ecosystems, the Great Barrier Reef has evolved to cope with many stresses: cyclones, droughts, floods, and many other natural fluctuations which cause the death of coral. The status of a coral reef is a fine balance between the rate of production of limestone and the rate of erosion and destruction. Studies of this balance and of change and growth in coral reefs involve many disciplines and are vital to our understanding of reef systems.

Many reef organisms gain their food by filtering it from the water mass. Numerous others reproduce by having their larvae float as plankton in the sea. Such organisms may be spawned on one reef, carried in the water mass for a number of weeks, and end up on another reef hundreds of kilometres away. Studies of water movements and the plankton communities of the Great Barrier Reef are aiding our understanding of the relationship between reefs.

ABOVE: *The commercial collecting of aquarium fish is an unusual use of Reef waters but, if properly controlled, provides a small industry without damage to fish populations.*

Another rewarding area of research relates to the biology and behaviour of the colourful reef fish, and this has yielded many interesting stories. For instance, many fish change sex at various times in their life cycle. For some fish colonies the normal social unit is one male and a number of females. If the male dies, the most dominant female changes to the male sex and the social unit carries on. In other cases, as with the popular coral trout, the fish when first mature are females, but when they get larger they change to males. This may have important implications for the management of fisheries for such species.

Human Impact on the Reefs

Australia is the only developed nation with significant expanses of coral reefs preserved in a relatively pristine state compared to those in overpopulated Third World countries where uncontrolled exploitation, bad land use practices and industrial pollution have spelt disaster for many reefs.

There is evidence that some of the reefs close to the mainland may have been slowly degraded over past decades by siltation. Low Isles off Port Douglas has deteriorated since the Royal Society Expedition almost 60 years ago, probably because of siltation from the mainland; parts of Green Island off Cairns have changed from being coral-dominated to being covered largely by seagrass and algae; fringing reefs around Magnetic Island just off Townsville have probably also deteriorated, perhaps from siltation resulting from dredging.

Although oil drilling has been prohibited in the Marine Park, oil pollution from shipping is an ever-present threat. Chronic low-level hydrocarbon pollution is a problem in most mainland harbours and, although levels of pesticides from sugarcane and other farms are very low, trace amounts of lindane and PCBs have been detected on the Reef.

The levels of nutrients (nitrates and phosphates) are naturally quite high in the nearshore reefs and there is some concern that sewage discharges from tourist resorts might cause them to become dangerously high, with the possible result of corals being replaced by algae.

During the late 1960s and early 1970s public concern for the future of the Great Barrier Reef became widespread. Specifically, public attention was focused on five main issues:

1 Conservation and preservation of the Reef for future generations
2 Deterioration of some parts of the Reef
3 Over-exploitation of the Reef's natural resources
4 Impact of pollutants
5 Threat posed by proposed oil drilling and mining

As a result of this public concern joint Commonwealth and Queensland Royal Commissions were established in 1970. Following that inquiry the Great Barrier Reef Marine Park Act was passed in 1975, formally ensuring the future wellbeing of the Reef through the establishment of a Marine Park covering an area of some 345 000 square kilometres.

The Act also established the Great Barrier Reef Marine Park Authority, a statutory body responsible for the planning, establishment and management of the Park.

The concept of the Marine Park is based on retaining a sustainable balance between Reef conservation and its use by fishermen, collectors, charter operators, tourists, scientists and others. Using the environment without abusing it is one of the key challenges and prerequisites for Reef managers and users alike.

BELOW: *Siltation from river outfalls can smother nearshore reefs and cause the death of corals. High levels of nutrients from farm fertilisers, washed into rivers and creeks, can also find their way into Reef waters.*

A Thorny Problem

Unlike the quaint little five-arm creatures that inhabit rock pools, the crown-of-thorns starfish (Acanthaster planci) is large (adults about 35-80 cm diameter), has up to 21 arms, is covered with venomous spines, and eats hard corals.

The crown-of-thorns digests its food externally; folds of its stomach are protruded from its mouth to envelop parts of the coral, enzymes are released and digested products are absorbed, leaving the white coral skeleton behind. This is soon colonised by algae. Each starfish may eat an area about the size of its central disc each day.

As in most starfish there is a planktonic stage that is important for dispersal. The sexes are separate and spawning may occur twice each summer. In a single spawning season, each female starfish may release as many as 100 million eggs into the water. This tiny, jelly-like larvae may drift in the plankton for 2-4 weeks. During this time they may be carried a distance of some 80 kilometres by the water currents. When the larvae have settled, they metamorphose into five-armed starfish about half a millimetre in size.

The early juveniles live beneath the surface of the reef—under boulders and rubble, on the dead bases of branching coral, and possibly in the deeper parts of reef slopes where they feed on pink coralline algae. Their diet switches to corals at the age of 6-12 months, when the starfish are 19-30 mm in diameter. The growth rate increases dramatically and they reach a diameter of about 150 mm at the age of 18 months, when they begin to leave their shelter and feed by day. It is only after starfish have undergone this change that outbreaks are generally first observed on reefs.

Crown-of-thorns Outbreaks

The oubreaks of the coral-eating crown-of-thorns starfish are one of the most serious issues in scientific research and management of the Great Barrier Reef. The starfish is usually an uncommon animal on reefs and causes little damage, but, sometimes for reasons not yet fully under-stood, the populations explode to many thousands or millions per reef and they may devastate a whole reef in 2-3 years.

In the past 25 years two series of outbreaks have affected mainly the central parts of the Great Barrier Reef. Similar outbreaks have occurred in Japan, South-East Asia, the Maldives, Micronesia, Samoa, Cook Islands, Hawaii, Fiji and on many other coral reefs in the Indo-Pacific.

The first outbreak recorded on the Great Barrier Reef was on Green Island reef off Cairns in 1962. Neighbouring reefs were also affected and during the next decade the outbreaks spread south to reefs off Innisfail, Townsville, Bowen and the northern Whitsundays. Outbreaks had virtually disappeared by the mid - 1970's.

The second wave was first noted on Green Island in 1979 and the major movement was again southwards, to Innisfail reefs in 1982, Townsville reefs in 1983-84 and Ayr-Bowen reefs in 1986-88.

The estimated percentage of reefs that have experienced outbreaks in the last 10 years over the entire Great Barrier Reef is between 13% and 21%. Many of these reefs show noticeable recovery of corals, although at the present time it is still quite patchy. It has been estimated that the fast growing branching, or staghorn, corals may recover completely within a couple of decades. Slow growing massive corals may take much longer to recover.

The Debate

In Australia, the crown-of-thorns starfish issue has aroused heated debate among scientists and the public. Opinion on the cause(s) is still divided, despite extensive research to resolve the question. Some scientists consider the outbreaks to be periodic natural events that had not been reported before the present boom in Reef tourism and scientific research. They argue that the amazing ability of relatively few starfish to produce many millions of offspring effectively predisposes the crown-of-thorns to sudden population explosions. Recent research has confirmed this ability. Others blame reef and adjacent land users in some way, for removing the predators of the starfish, disturbing the Reef, or polluting the seas.

Controls

As we do not yet know whether the outbreaks are entirely natural, the result of human activities or result from a combination of all these factors, controls are limited to small-scale tactical programs on reefs of special importance to tourism or scientific research. So far any large-scale attempts to control the starfish have been unsuccessful. Trials have been carried out on a number of reefs using Navy divers to collect starfish, or alternatively, inject them with poison. However, none of these successfully protected the corals as starfish from surrounding areas moved into cleared areas. The Great Barrier Reef Marine Park Authority belives that it would be foolhardy to interfere too much in the life of the Reef system before the starfish problem is more fully understood. If outbreaks are a natural part of the ecology of the Reef, then they are likely to play an important role in this ecosystem, similar to the role bushfires have in structuring and maintaining the biological diversity of the Australian bush.

Finding the Answers

Rather than devote resources to costly and highly dubious manual eradication, the Authority has promoted scientific research on the starfish to examine its biology and ecology and determine the reasons for the outbreaks. A major, coordinated research program into the starfish phenomenon has been underway since 1985. This program has included studies into the reproduction, larval nutrition and dispersal, and the recruitment of the starfish. In addition, investigations into both the role of predators in controlling starfish populations and coral recovery following outbreaks are being carried out.

The primary aim of the research program is to determine the cause(s) of the observed outbreaks. Research over recent years has made significant contributions to our understanding not only of the starfish but of the entire coral reef ecosystem.

OPPOSITE: *The crown-of-thorns starfish, Acanthaster planci has been known in the Reef region for a long time, but was considered rare prior to the population explosion of the 1960s.*
TOP LEFT: *Control of the crown-of-thorns starfish has been attempted on an experimental level by injection with copper sulphate, however no large-scale control program has yet been effective.*
TOP RIGHT: *Adult crown-of-thorns starfish sometimes eat algae but prefer coral.*
INSET: *This giant triton is one of the few confirmed predators of the crown-of-thorns starfish.*

L. Zann/G.B.R.M.P.A.

L. Zell/G.B.R.M.P.A.

G. Bull/G.B.R.M.P.A.

Looking After Tomorrow

To assist in managing the huge area of the Marine Park, it has been divided into four sections, each with its own zoning plan.

Through the use of zoning, conflicting activities are separated; areas are provided which are suitable for particular activities and some areas are protected from various uses. Levels of protection and/or use within the Park vary from zones where almost any legal activity can occur to zones of almost total exclusion.

The only activities which are prohibited throughout the Park are oil exploration, mining (other than for scientific purposes), littering and the taking of large specimens of certain species of fish.

The Authority is very dependent on the input of reef users, individuals and organisations in reviewing and preparing zoning plans.

Each zoning plan is intended to be reviewed as soon as practicable after it has been in operation for five years or so. A new Cairns plan was launched in April 1992 after extensive public participation in the review. The Far Northern Section Zoning Plan is next for consideration.

Far Northern Section

The Far northern Section extends for over 700 kilometres from just north of Lizard Island, northwards to the tip of Cape York, and covers approximately 83 000 square kilometres. It has been fully operational since February 1986.

The most remote section in the Marine Park, its fauna are both diverse and abundant. Thirty species of birds and an estimated 1000 species of fish occur within the outer boundaries of the section.

The area is best known for its rich fishing grounds. Prawn trawling and barramundi netting are significant commercial ventures while charter boat operations for fishing and diving are a popular and increasing activity.

Cairns Section

The Cairns Section extends for over 400 kilometres from Dunk Island in the south, northwards past Cairns and Cooktown to Lizard Island, and covers approximately 35 000 square kilometres.

Twenty-two species of seabirds have been recorded on islands within the outer boundaries of the Cairns Section, and Michaelmas Cay is recognised as one of the most important seabird nesting sites in Queensland.

The area is best known for its prolific fishing grounds and long-established tourist facilities. Prawn trawling is a significant commercial fishery while game fishing, especially for giant black marlin, is a popular tourist activity.

Central Section

The Central Section of the Marine Park extends from the southern end of the Whitsunday Islands to Dunk Island in the north. It covers an area of about 77 000 square kilometres.

The marine life found within the Central Section is varied and abundant. Approximately 1500 species of fish occur in the section, many becoming prey to the 22 species of seabirds that permanently inhabit or regularly

ABOVE: *Sea planes provide an unusual and interesting way of exploring the Reef. Their use is controlled to ensure they do not disturb nesting birds.*

migrate into the section. The reefs in the area include over 400 species of corals.

This section is adjacent to one of the most populated parts of the north Queensland coast and so user activities abound. The area is known for its rich fishing grounds, exciting dive sites and tourist facilities. Tourism is rapidly expanding and, together with commercial fisheries, is of major economic importance to the region.

Marine research is also important in the section because of the proximity of two major marine research centres (the Australian Institute of Marine Science and James Cook University of North Queensland).

Mackay/Capricorn Section

This section is by far the largest in the Marine Park, covering an area of 137 000 square kilometres. It stretches along the coast from Bundaberg in the south to the Whitsundays in the north and extends seawards some 300 kilometres at its widest point.

The section contains many well-known reefs and islands. The Capricorn-Bunker group of islands and reefs contains the largest and best known group of true coral cay islands in the Marine Park.

Uses in this section vary from tourist operations to commercial fishing and most of these activities have been well established in the area for many years. This part of the Reef has been a focus for scientific research for almost 100 years and has scientific research stations established on Heron Island and One Tree Island.

The area is well known as a turtle and seabird nesting site with hundreds of visitors to the various islands each year to witness these events.

Beyond 2000

While the primary responsibility for looking after the Great Barrier Reef as a World Heritage Area lies with the Great Barrier Reef Marine Park Authority, many other individuals and organisations are concerned with its use and care about its future.

A significant milestone in 1992 was the development of a 25 Year Strategic Plan for the Area by representatives of different management, user and interest groups.

This Plan has established directions for the Reef's reasonable use and conservation into the 21st century.

88

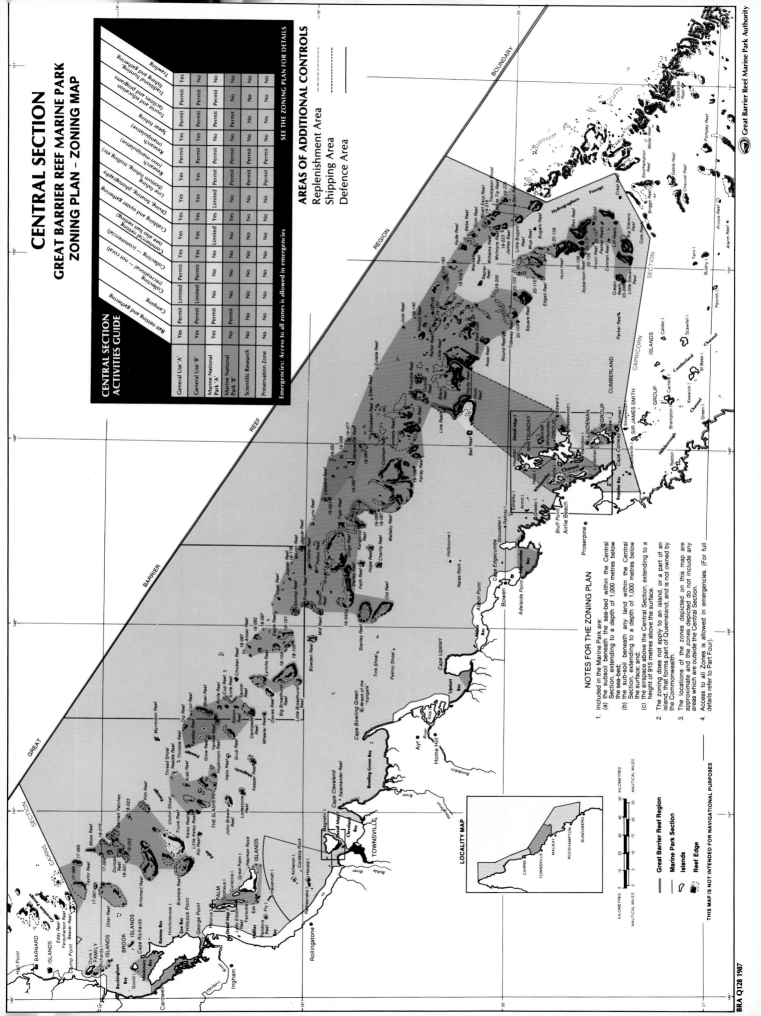

CENTRAL SECTION
GREAT BARRIER REEF MARINE PARK
ZONING PLAN – ZONING MAP

CENTRAL SECTION ACTIVITIES GUIDE

	Bait netting and gathering	Camping	Collecting (recreational) — not coral	Collecting (commercial) — not coral	Commercial netting (see also bait netting)	Crabbing and oyster gathering	Diving, boating, photography	Line fishing, trolling etc.	Research (bottom fishing, trolling etc.)	Research (non-manipulative)	Research (manipulative)	Spear fishing	Tourist and education facilities and programs	Traditional hunting, fishing and gathering	Trawling
General Use 'A'	Yes	Limited	Permit	Yes	Yes	Yes	Yes	Yes	Yes	Yes	Permit	Yes	Yes	Yes	Yes
General Use 'B'	Permit	Limited	Permit	Yes	Limited	Yes	Yes	Yes	Yes	Yes	Permit	Permit	Permit	No	No
Marine National Park 'A'	Permit	No	No	No	No	Limited	Yes	Yes	Permit	Yes	Permit	No	Permit	No	No
Marine National Park 'B'	No	No	No	No	No	No	Yes	No	No	Yes	Permit	No	Permit	No	No
Scientific Research	No	No	No	No	No	No	No	No	No	No	Permit	No	Permit	No	No
Preservation Zone	No	No	No	No	No	No	No	No	No	No	Permit	No	Permit	No	No

Emergencies: Access to all zones is allowed in emergencies

SEE THE ZONING PLAN FOR DETAILS

AREAS OF ADDITIONAL CONTROLS

Replenishment Area
Shipping Area
Defence Area

NOTES FOR THE ZONING PLAN

1. Included in the Marine Park are:
   (a) the subsoil beneath the sea-bed within the Central Section, extending to a depth of 1,000 metres below the sea-bed;
   (b) the sub-soil beneath any land within the Central Section, extending to a depth of 1,000 metres below the surface; and
   (c) the airspace above the Central Section, extending to a height of 915 metres above the surface.

2. The zoning does not apply to an island, or a part of an island, that forms part of Queensland, and is not owned by the Commonwealth.

3. The locations of the zones depicted on this map are approximate and the zones depicted do not include any areas which are outside the Central Section.

4. Access to all Zones is allowed in emergencies. (For full details refer to Part Four).

LOCALITY MAP

KILOMETRES
NAUTICAL MILES

THIS MAP IS NOT INTENDED FOR NAVIGATIONAL PURPOSES

Great Barrier Reef Region
Marine Park Section
Islands
Reef Edge

KILOMETRES
NAUTICAL MILES

Great Barrier Reef Marine Park Authority

BRA Q128 1987

7 A WINDOW ON THE REEF

Just imagine, you can travel to the bottom of the sea to experience the wonderful sights of the Great Barrier Reef, not by boat or submarine but as the fish see it!

At the aquarium in Townsville's Great Barrier Reef Wonderland you can observe the colourful coral and sea creatures just as if you were a deep sea diver or predator shark but without even getting wet.

Gordon Claridge/A.N.T. Photo Library

The aquarium gives you the feeling of being underwater while allowing you to share your experiences with others.

TOP INSET: Young and old discover unusual Reef creatures in the touch pool. Sea stars are particular favourites.

BOTTOM INSET: Close to the heart of Townsville and to other tourist attractions, the Great Barrier Reef Aquarium brings the Reef

G.B.R.M.P.A.

G B R Aquarium

The Great Barrier Reef Aquarium

The concept of the large coral reef aquarium was initiated by Graeme Kelleher, Chairman of the Great Barrier Reef Marine Park Authority, and supported by the people of Townsville and the Commonwealth and Queensland governments. The Wonderland complex was opened in June 1987. In addition to the aquarium, the complex includes the first omnimax theatre in the Southern Hemisphere, the Museum of Tropical Queensland which is a regional branch of the Queensland Museum, a promenade of retail shops, the Marine Park Authority's administrative offices and departure points for vessels that go to the Reef and nearby Magnetic Island.

Designed as an educational facility, the aquarium encourages visitors to learn about the Reef, and explore it with a greater understanding and appreciation.

A Reef Replica

Building a reef environment on land relied on many years of research and special technology to be able to simulate a coral reef. Natural elements including 700 tonnes of limestone rock, 200 tonnes of sand, and nearly 3 million litres of sea water went into the formation of the reef foundation. The actual design resembles a cross-section through a typical reef and incorporates a reef front, reef flat and lagoon. Once the framework was complete the fish, corals and other living organisms were added to complete the formula for a miniature coral reef ecosystem. All the living animals and plants were collected from locations within the Great Barrier Reef region.

Reef-building corals, algae, plankton and a wide range of herbivorous and carnivorous animals were essential to the reef community and important parts of the food chain. Algae were established first to form the basis of the food chain. The corals were then collected and attached to the limestone rocks in locations best suited to the light and water current requirements of each species. Gradually the reef came alive.

Water currents are created by recirculating water through large return pipes and waves are formed with the aid of a wave machine, driven by air pressure, at one end of the coral reef. This movement of water is vitally important in the circulation of food and oxygen and in moving waste products through the water purification system.

The Algal Turf Farm

The aquarium is a closed system. Tank water is recycled and water purification takes place using the nutrient-absorbing behaviour of marine algae. The system was developed by Dr Walter Adey at the Smithsonian Instiute's Marine Systems Laboratory. The algal turf scrubbers recreate the same processes which occur in nature by using the photosynthetic action of marine algae to purify the sea water.

An algal turf scrubber consists of a shallow tray measuring about 2 m x 1 m and containing two thin, plastic screens. Every 20 seconds a tip bucket releases a swish of water from the reef exhibit across the screens. Algae growing on the screens remove the waste products

G.B.R.M.P.A.

Gordon Claridge/A.N.T. Photo Library

ABOVE: *Stocking the tank with rock, corals and other marine life was a painstaking job. The exact conditions of the Reef have been duplicated — including tides, waves and an algal turf filtration system. The aquarium is an important part of the program to educate people about the Great Barrier Reef Marine Park.*

92

produced by the fish and other tank inhabitants and help to maintain normal oxygen and acidity levels in the tank water.

The alga 'turf' on the screens grows rapidly under these conditions. Every seven to twenty days the turf is harvested and discarded taking with it the tank wastes. Like other plants, the algae require plenty of sunlight to photosynthesise. For those days when there is very little sunlight, large bright overhead lights can be activated. These lights are also used at night to extend the period of photosynthesis.

The Living Reef

The aquarium reef houses over 1000 coral colonies made up of nearly 150 hard and soft coral species. Several hundred varieties of reef fish are represented.

Fish and corals are not the only animals at home in the tank. A wide range of invertebrates live in the reef exhibit as they do in the wild. Such fascinating animals as sea cucumbers, anemones, starfish, molluscs and giant clams add further interest as they play their roles in the only living coral reef in captivity.

The biological community of the reef exhibit is planned to be as self-maintaining as the natural

ABOVE: *From the air the size of the aquarium is apparent. Compare it with the yachts moored in the Ross Creek.*

environment of the Reef. All the inhabitants find their own food and no artificial food is added. So successful has been the creation of this reef on land that many animals, including the corals, have reproduced just as they would on the Reef.

Predators on Parade

No aquarium would be complete without sharks! The predator exhibit is directly opposite the reef exhibit separated by a transparent tunnel through which visitors walk. The two tanks are separated so that the large predators are kept out of the reef exhibit. Can you imagine what would happen if the sharks were let loose in the reef exhibit? Predator exhibit water is filtered through a separate algal turf farm but, unlike the reef exhibit, the predator exhibit does not have wave action.

All the predators are fed regularly every few days and are not expected to live on a reef-reliant food chain as are the animals in the reef exhibit.

93

Humbug fish
Orange-tailed damselfish
Puller fish

Ned Kelly/G.B.R.M.P.A.

ABOVE: *The aquarium makes the Reef and the Marine Park more accessible to the public, and many school programs have been established so that children of all ages get the most out of their visit.*

The predator exhibit is home to black-tip whaler or reef sharks, a leopard shark and sea turtle as well as numerous large fish.

Through extensive displays, visitors of all ages can learn more about the Reef. Hands-on activities, feature talks, computer displays and videos stimulate a better understanding of the Reef.

A multi-screen audiovisual program in the aquarium theatrette provides the visitor with a very thorough introduction to coral reef ecology. This presentation not only fills you in on some coral reef basics, but puts you in a mood for discovery and learning.

The aquarium's galleries feature colourful underwater photographs, with many of the subjects passing by in real colour just centimetres away in the reef exhibit.

Appreciation of the aquarium's unique coral reef environment is made easy by the huge viewing windows on three sides of the reef tank. The 20 metre long acrylic tunnel separating the coral reef and predator exhibits creates an underwater feeling and provides a 180 degree view into the busy life of the reef. From here you can see parrotfish chomping on algal-covered rocks and giant

clams sucking water in and out of their mantle cavity.

From vantage points like the tunnel, aquarium guides explain the characteristics of various animals and answer questions.

Numerous smaller display aquariums give visitors even closer views of reef life, from colourful anemone fish to the poisonous stonefish.

A Living Classroom

School programs have been established so that children of all ages get the most out of their visit to the aquarium. A discovery room has been set up to give them a closer look at marine creatures.

A touch pool provides an experience that most children (or adults) won't forget. A shallow tank, less than 40 cm in depth and below a six-year-old's waist in height, the touch pool allows everyone to discover the feel of the Reef. It is delightful to see how visitors react to the touch of a leathery blue starfish or the smooth slimy surface of a sea cucumber.

The Great Barrier Reef Aquarium makes the Reef and the Marine Park more accessible to the public, by conveying essential information and providing unique insights and experiences.

The Great Barrier Reef is one of the world's most precious possessions. A visit to the aquarium gives people an opportunity to learn about the Reef and appreciate its special need, as the wourld's largest marine park, for conservation and management.

Index

Numbers in italics indicate illustrations

A

Aborigines 12, 58, 66, *10, 66*
Abudefduf 54
Acanthaster 63, 86, *87*
Acanthuridae 61
Acropora 30, 34
Aipysurus 58
Alexander Reef 23
Algae (see also Zooxanthellae and
  species names)
  24, 30, 36, *36, 37*
America (ship) 74
Amphiprion 32
Amusium 81
Anemones 31, 62, *12, 39, 44*
Anemone fish *12, 32, 45*
Angel fish *6*
Aquaculture 40
Aquarium 90, 92-94, *90-91,92-94*
Arothron 43, 63
Ascidians 50, *51*
Australian Institue of Marine Science 33
Australian Museum 54

B

Barnacles *45*
Beach rock 20
Birds 20, 57, *56, 57*
Bleaching (of corals) 33
Booby *56*
Borers 30
Brain coral 34
Brittle stars *49*
Bryozoans 52
Butterfly cod *61*
Butterfly fish *27*

C

Cape Tribulation 23, *22*
Caretta 12
Catamarans 9
Casuarina 17
Cays 18, 20
Caulerpa 36, *36*
Chaetodontidae *6, 55*
Charter boats *80*
Chelonia 12, *59*
Chironex 62, *62*
Chlorodesmis 36, *37*

Ciguatera 63
Climate 36
Clams 40, *30, 70*
Coelenterata (see also names of
  groups and species) 44
Commercial fishing 9, 81, *81*
Cone shells 62
Conservation 85, 88
Continental shelf 18
Cook, James 64, 66-68, 72, *66*
Cooktown 23
Copepods 44
Coralline algae 30
Coral cod *55*
Corals (see also species name)
  9, 30-36, *34, 35*
Cowries 28, 47
Crinoids *44, 50*
Crown-of-thorns starfish 62, 86, *87*
Crustacea (see also names of groups
  and species) 44
Cyclones 20, 24
Cyerce 30

D

Dardanus 6
Dictyosphaeria 37
Diving *10, 83*
Dragonfish *26*
Dugong 9, 12, 59, *13,59,66*
Dunk Island 23

E

Echinoderms (see also names of
  groups and individual species) 48
Economics 80, 81
Ecosystem 26
Eels *62*
Egretta 56
Endangered animals 9
Endeavour (ship, 66-68, *65, 73*
Endeavour Reef *68*
Energy 38
Epinephalus 54
Expeditions 71
Exploration 66, 67, 71

F

Feather stars *44, 50*
Ferguson (ship) *76*
Fire coral 62

First aid 62
Fish (see also names of groups and
  species)
  9, 30, 54, 60, 62, *26-27, 54, 55, 60,
  63*
Fishing 9, 81, 82, *81, 82*
Flatworms *38, 53*
Finders, Matthew 64, 69, 71, 72, *69*
Foam (ship) 74
Food chains 38
Freshwater 20, 23, 24
Fringing reefs 18, 22, 23, 24, *22*

G

Game fishing 82
Glaucus 10
Goatfish *39*
Golden City (ship) 74
Gorgonians *26, 44*
Gothenberg (ship) 74, *74*
Great Barrier Reef; age 18, 20;
  diversity 11, 24, 28, 42; from space
  6; from the air 6; 16
Great Barrier Reef Marine Park
  Authority 14, 78, 92
Great Barrier Reef Wonderland 90, 92-
  94, *90-94*
Green Island *17*
Guano 20

H

Halimeda 30, 36, *37*
Hardy Reef *18*
Hermit crabs *7, 45*
Heron Island *78*
Hexabranchus 46
Hinchinbrook Island 23
Historic Shipwrecks Act 77
Holothurians *49*
Hoskyn Reef *21*
Human impact 85
Humpback whales 9, *13*
Hydrozoans *10, 62*

I

Ice age 16, 18
Investigator (ship) 69
Islands (see also Cays) 22; number 9

J

James Cook University 40

95